Brewing for Cornwall

A Family Tradition

The Story of St Austell Brewery

1851-2001

written by Liz Luck

I feel no pain dear mother now
But oh, I am so dry!
O take me to a brewery
And leave me there to die.

First published in Great Britain in 2001
by St Austell Brewery Co. Ltd.
63 Trevarthian Road, St Austell, Cornwall PL25 4BY

ISBN 0-9540537-0-2

Printed by St Ives Roche Ltd, St Austell, Cornwall PL26 8LX
Main photography by Julian Essam, other photographs with kind permission of the National Trust in Cornwall,
Royal Institution of Cornwall, Scottish Brewing Archive, Tuckers Maltings, H.Tempest Ltd, Keith Salmon and
members of the family and Brewery employees.
Design by Laurence Sutherland.

CONTENTS

OPPOSITE: *Black Head with St Austell in the distance.* ABOVE: *Walter Hicks invoice from 1890, courtesy of Cornwall Records Office.*

ST. JAMES'S PALACE

As one of a small number of independent family brewers left in Britain, the St. Austell Brewery has grown steadily from the initial vision of a young Cornishman called Walter Hicks in 1851 to become one of the largest private companies in Cornwall. With its distinctive black and gold paintwork adorning its public houses, and the historic brewery itself up on the hill above St. Austell still brewing beers known to earlier generations, St. Austell Brewery has become part of the fabric of Cornwall.

The Company makes a notable contribution to the rural communities of Cornwall - and Devon - through its ownership of local pubs and its investment in their future. It has played its part in the local economy for over 150 years as a large and reliable employer and represents, with its continuing emphasis on the quality of hospitality, an important contribution to the tourist industry on which Cornwall relies so heavily.

On the occasion of St. Austell Brewery's 150th anniversary, I would like to send my congratulations to its staff, management and tenants, all of whom form part of a great Cornish success story.

Walter Hicks, founder of St Austell Brewery.

Introduction

Who was Walter Hicks, and why should we remember him? The name might be familiar to devotees of a strong Cornish ale called Hicks Special Draught, they might even have noticed its pump clip which for many years bore the slightly melancholy image of a sombre bearded man with a high starched Victorian collar, but as to who he was - well what does it matter, as long as the beer tastes good?

Cornwall was an extraordinary place to be in the early nineteenth century, and much of the structure of our lives today has its origins in this period which was a ferment of energy and innovation. Philip Payton, in his definitive history *Cornwall*, describes it thus: *'The heady mix of Trevithick and Davy, Lemon and Fox, Basset and Williams, Treffry and Gilbert, Bickford and Gurney, made for an astonishing concentration of intellectual activity and inventiveness...Cornish society became remarkably self-confident and assertive, and Cornishness was expressed increasingly in terms of technological and scientific advance.'* He goes on to describe how a new breed of Cornish industrialist emerged alongside the practical engineers: *'These industrialists - capitalists, innovators, inventors, reformers - brought a particular single-mindedness and determination which prompted the redefinition of Cornish society as modern and progressive, and which helped mould a re-defining Cornish identity based on industrial prowess.'* Out of this intoxicating crucible came Walter Hicks: not an extraordinary man, no visionary or genius, but the embodiment of his age - he was Typical Victorian Man and he was going to Found something.

The business he founded, on the principles of sound finance, paternalistic care for his workforce and a fascination with cutting-edge industrial technology, is today one of Cornwall's leading private companies. It directly employs some 885 people, owns more than 150 public houses and hotels in Cornwall and Devon and has an annual turnover of around £50 million, yet it remains as it has always been at heart - a family concern. It strides the national stage as one of just a handful of vigorous and independent regional breweries to have survived the years of take-over and amalgamation which almost killed off the traditional British brewery. Locally it is a beneficiary of, as well as a contributor to, the cultural distinctiveness of Cornwall. No company so closely identified with such a high-profile, recognisable region of Britain could fail to benefit from the association, but it has also added to Cornwall's reputation for distinction and quality through its intrinsic commitment to high standards and a strong visual and local identity.

The business he founded has been called St Austell Brewery since 1934, but 150 years ago it had no name; it was simply a young Cornishman called Walter Hicks malting barley in a shed at Trenance.

The First and Last Inn, Sennen. Leased to the Brewery from 1935-1978.

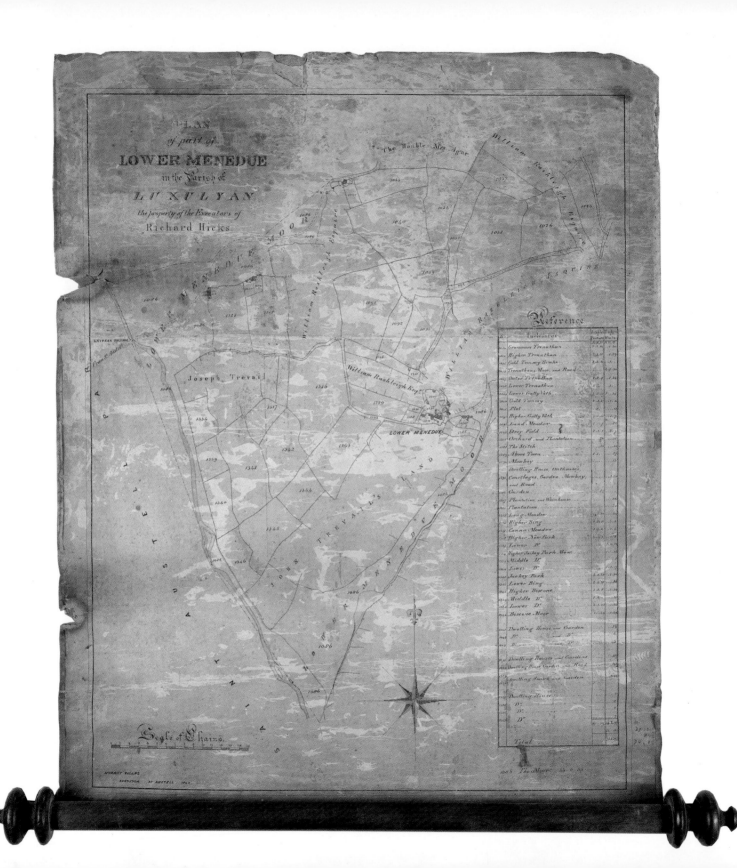

PLAN
of part of
LOWER MENEDUE
in the Parish of
LUXULYAN
the property of the Executors of
Richard Hicks.

LOWER MENEDUE

Reference

Scale of Chains

Total

CHAPTER I

The beginnings

Walter's early life is somewhat obscure. He was baptised at Luxulyan Church on January 30th 1829, the first-born son of a 75-year-old yeoman farmer called Richard Hicks and his young second wife Frances (née Warn). Richard and Frances lived at Lower Menadue, then a large farming settlement on the rough rocky fringes of moorland between Bugle and Luxulyan, clustered on the lower slopes of the hill from which it took its Cornish name (*meneth du* - the Black Hill).

There had been Hickses at Menadue for many generations. This was never rich farming land - A.L. Rowse described it

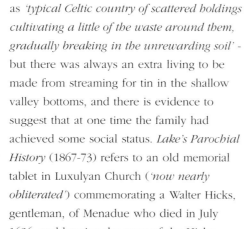

as *'typical Celtic country of scattered holdings cultivating a little of the waste around them, gradually breaking in the unrewarding soil'* - but there was always an extra living to be made from streaming for tin in the shallow valley bottoms, and there is evidence to suggest that at one time the family had achieved some social status. *Lake's Parochial History* (1867-73) refers to an old memorial tablet in Luxulyan Church (*'now nearly obliterated'*) commemorating a Walter Hicks, gentleman, of Menadue who died in July 1636, and bearing the arms of the Hicks family described as *'Or, a castle triple towered between three battle axes sable'*.

Richard Hicks's first marriage, to his father's housekeeper Elizabeth Pascoe, had been childless and perhaps it was with a mixture of relief and some surprise that he swiftly married Frances Warn on November 13th 1828, not long before the birth of his son. Walter was just six years old, however, and his sister Frances Bersey Hicks three, when their father died in February 1835. What happened to

Walter after this is not entirely clear but it seems likely that he never again lived permanently at his ancestral home, which was subsequently farmed by tenants. A year later his mother married a man called John Miller, and went on to have two more children whilst living at Bridges in Luxulyan. The 1841 census return, however, records Walter and Frances Hicks, aged twelve and nine and mysteriously described as *'independent'*, living with the Nicholls family at Lestoon on the other side of the valley from Menadue; the Millers are not to be found. The Nicholls family was related to Walter through his grandfather, and this would fit in with Hicks family tradition which has it that both Walter's father and mother died when he was young and thereafter he was cared for by assorted aunts.

The next time Walter reappears in our view is in the 1851 census as a young man of 22. Now he is living as a boarder at Trenance Farm to the north-west of St Austell, on the high ridge of land between the Gover and Trenance valleys. Walter's landlady was Phillippa Andrew, widow of George Andrew and described as a farmer of 166 acres; also amongst the household at Trenance at that time was her 13-year-old step-daughter Caroline who was later to become Walter's second wife.

Walter is described in the census as a landed proprietor, but shortly afterwards, probably in the autumn of 1851, he set up in business as a maltster. It is clear that the Andrew family (sometimes written 'Andrews') had a significant influence on Walter's life; not only did he marry two of them - first cousins - but it is also likely that it was their

OPPOSITE: *Map of Lower Menadue Farm, 1842.* ABOVE: *Modern replacement of old memorial tablet in Luxulyan Church.* RIGHT: *Caroline Hicks, née Andrew.*

involvement in the malting business as well as farming (George and Henry Andrew were registered as maltsters in Fore Street in 1844 and 1847) that led Walter to venture into this particular profession. Family tradition has it that to finance the endeavour he took out a mortgage of £1500 on Lower Menadue, probably with the East Cornwall Bank (Robins, Foster, Coode and Bolitho, later to become Barclays) in St Austell. The exact location of Walter's first malt house is unknown, but it was somewhere in the Trenance area - either at the farm or nearby in the valley.

There is no evidence to suggest that Walter was brewing at this stage, but as he would have supplied malt to many of the ale-houses and inns in and around St Austell which brewed their own beer, no doubt he was gaining valuable insights into the business. Within ten years Walter had married Emma, daughter of the St Austell draper Benjamin Andrew, and had moved his business to Church Street in the centre of the town, just down from the White Hart Hotel. By now he was trading as a wine and spirit merchant as well as a maltster, and it was not long before he had driven his local competitors (initially six maltsters and three wine and spirit merchants) out of business.

Walter might well have first tried his hand at the art of brewing in 1863 after buying the lease of the Seven Stars Inn, with its own small brew house, but it seems likely that his sights had always been set on building St Austell's first modern commercial-scale brewery. Within a year he had begun the long and tortuous process of buying the old London Inn on Market Street; due to its complicated shared ownership it was a process that was to take him until 1870 to complete. This site was worth waiting for: the inn itself had sixteen rooms, a large cellar, and a brew house, yard, stable and loft, but the extensive site he eventually secured also included land running uphill towards the station, where he later built Tregarne House, and property

RIGHT AND CENTRE RIGHT: *Tuckers Maltings, Newton Abbott.*
FAR RIGHT: *Tregonissey House in 1989.*

Malting

Malt is where it all begins. Barley is one of the four crucial ingredients in the brewing of traditional British beers, along with hot water ('liquor'), hops and yeast. The malting process enables the carbohydrate in the barley to be easily released so that fermentation may then convert it to alcohol. Traditional malt houses of this period needed a large well-ventilated floor area and a strong construction to support the weight of tanks filled with liquid. Walter's first malt house might have been a small operation, but it would have been an easily recognisable building with a long, low profile, repetitive fenestration and a distinctive, perhaps conical, kiln roof.

The process involves steeping the barley in water for up to 70 hours during which time germination begins. The grain is then spread out on the malting floor and turned regularly to maintain an even temperature and prevent the shoots from knitting together. During the final stage the part-germinated grain is kiln dried to stop growth and imbue it with colour and flavour. It is now *'no longer hard and steely but crisp and crunchy like a good biscuit'* (George Luck, see below). Barley has become malt.

In the winter of 1932-3 George Luck, later to become Managing Director of St Austell Brewery, worked at a maltings in Bath as part of his training as a brewer. The process he describes here would have changed little from that in Walter's day: *'We started work at 4.30am. That meant leaving my digs at 4, always in pitch dark of course and usually, or so it seemed, in ice or snow. (In those days, before efficient air conditioning, malting was only undertaken in the winter months because of the difficulty of temperature control in the summer during germination of the grain.) The first job was turning and aerating the grain on the kilns before finally unloading them. This was a hot job and a sulphurous one too from the fumes of the coke fires below. The rest of the morning was spent in turning the floors, gradually thickening the depth and then reducing it again later. This was done with large flat wooden shovels. It was hard work, very good for the development of forearm muscles, and also quite skilled, requiring a twist to throw the grain out in a wide spray, for the "piece" as it was called had to finish completely smooth and even - no lumps or ridges. No-one else was allowed on the "piece" I was given so that when George or sometimes Harold [Thompson] came round, the Foreman could truthfully report "that is all his own work".'*

on Market Hill which he was to use for offices and a malt house. In 1869 he began to build his new Steam Brewery, and a house for his growing family, on the main site of the London Inn just up the hill from the parish church.

This grand building, with its classical brick façade and rows of identical round-headed windows fronting Market Street, is known today as Tregonissey House. You can still recognise certain features that identify its origins as a brewery, including the louvered ventilation lantern on the roof ridge and a distinctively massive chimney. In using steam to heat the mash instead of direct heating by furnaces (hence the proud appellation 'Steam Brewery') and a new form of refrigeration system, Walter Hicks took advantage of the innovations in the brewing industry that swept the country in the 1870s. There is no doubt that his enthusiasm for, and knowledge of, technological advances helped to create what was even by national standards a truly modern brewery; it must have been the talk of the county. In a detailed description that appeared in the *West Briton* in 1870, we are told that it consisted of *'four stories, the upper being fitted with three bins each capable of containing 100 bushels of malt, also two furnaces sufficiently large to hold 2,000 and 1,000 gallons. By a new and admirable apparatus the mashing is most successfully carried on. The next floor has two large receivers. After the beer has been boiled it is poured into these vessels in which it passes to the next flat and immediately falls on a patent refrigerator. This ingenious and useful appliance is made of a number of copper tubes perpendicularly set, through which cold water is constantly flowing, as soon as the beer drops off it is then passed at its*

required temperature into the vats...The brewery is well supplied with spring water which is pumped by a steam engine of 3hp. The cellar is very capacious.'

Such was the brewery's success, however, that within twenty years Walter and his son were looking for a site outside the confines of the town on which to build a new and much larger brewery.

A gentlemanly trade

Why did Walter Hicks choose to become a brewer? For a young man with social ambitions and a fascination with the innovations of Victorian Britain, brewing was a business with excellent prospects. Had Walter grown up at Lower Menadue he would perhaps have followed his father into farming (although the long-standing agricultural depression in Cornwall, which culminated in the failure of the potato crop in the 'Hungry Forties', might have made him think twice) but everything changed for him when his ancestral ties to the land were severed at the age of six.

The retailing of alcohol was generally considered a scurrilous occupation, particularly with the rise of the temperance movement in the nineteenth century. In 1913 the *St Austell Star* reported a heated discussion amongst members of the Urban Council over plans that had been submitted for an off-licence in Duke Street. Mr Pascoe quoted the popular moral ditty *'This is the gin shop - all glittering and gay - which helps our brothers, weak mortals, astray',* before going on to say that *'he would rather this particular trade hid its head than make itself too prominent'.* The proposed building had, he felt, *'too much window space for the display of liquors'* (whereupon one of his more irreverent colleagues suggested that perhaps the glass could be frosted...).

However, this widespread opprobrium did not extend to commercial brewing. Indeed, as Lynn Pearson tells us in her fascinating book *British Breweries: an Architectural History,* it was overwhelmingly seen as *'a suitable occupation for gentlemen'.* As to why brewers were more socially acceptable than other Victorian industrialists, she concludes wryly that although the partial removal of the human element from practical brewing through mechanisation might have had an effect (the gentleman brewers did not have to get their hands dirty), no doubt equally telling was their capacity to make enormous profits.

'At the foot of Menacuddle Hill started an institution of which St Austell has reason to be proud, Walter Hicks's brewery. As a regrettable teetotaller I cannot personally witness to the excellence of its beverages, as to which there is better and consistent testimony from all over Cornwall. But the heavy, sweet, soporific odour of hops and malt from the brewery up the hill is a constant reminder of schooldays, as I find is the case with many others beside me - there is nothing so nostalgic as scents and smells.' A.L. Rowse *St Austell: Church, Town and Parish* (1960).

ABOVE: *Walter, Caroline and their children in the old Brewery House garden (now Tregarne Terrace) c.1888.* OPPOSITE: *Clay workers, Blackpool Pit.*

Entrepreneurs were also increasingly attracted to what was an ancient trade in which scientific practice was beginning to replace some of its traditional mystique. The pace of change is reflected in the number of British patent applications concerning brewing and malting: in the 1860s there were 40 a year being received, in contrast to 27 for the entire decade of the 1830s. Walter loved his mod cons, and he had a desire to rise socially through the hot cauldron of opportunity that was Victorian industrial society; he was made to be a brewer.

Wealth from white gold

St Austell is not one of Cornwall's ancient towns. For most of its history it was a 'church-town' - just a cluster of cottages around the fine old parish church, with its remarkable carvings on the tower and outside walls - and the natural meeting place for a large rural parish. Despite a sudden growth in the eighteenth century due to a boom in tin and copper mining at the Polgooth and, later, Crinnis mines nearby, it was still being described in 1842 as *'a poor town, but the parish is populous'*. In 1851 when Walter Hicks was setting up in business the population of the parish was 10,750, of which only about 4,000 lived in the town, in comparison to Truro's urban population of 16,316. St Austell, however, was on the brink of a transformation.

There can be no doubt that a key factor in the meteoric success of Walter's business, along with his personal qualities as a shrewd businessman and technophile, was simply being in the right place at the right time. The second half of the nineteenth century saw the chill of dereliction and depression stealing through Cornwall, as the decline in tin and copper mining and its associated industries moved inexorably eastwards, but St Austell was protected from its harshest effects by the economic power of 'white gold'.

Back in the 1780s the Devonian chemist William Cookworthy had discovered huge reserves of china clay in Cornwall, particularly in the Hensbarrow granite moors north of St Austell. The industry developed gradually, in a localised and piecemeal fashion, until by the 1850s it was producing 65,000 tons a year and employing some 7,000 men, women and children in the St Austell area. The output then rose dramatically to more than 550,000 tons by the end of the century. This expansion was spurred on by the discovery of a multitude of uses for this curious decomposed granite far beyond its original use in the manufacture of porcelain - notably in the production of paper, paint, cosmetics and medicines.

By 1883 St Austell was considered to be *'much improved through modernising and the erection of new buildings'*, and a visitor commented that *'its commerce in various branches is very considerable, and its inhabitants are in general remarked for being an industrious and thriving people'*.

CHAPTER II

The new brewery

Much had happened to Walter Hicks in the forty years since he started work as a maltster. Step by step with the success of his business went his growth in stature as a citizen. His family had grown too; by 1890 he had ten children and was looking for somewhere larger than the Brewery House (part of Tregonissey House) to live. His wife Emma had died of tuberculosis in 1863, having borne two daughters, and the following year he married her cousin Caroline Andrew - that 13-year-old girl from Trenance Farm who was now a handsome woman of 26. Walter and Caroline had nine children between 1865 and 1880 - two boys and seven girls (one, Mary, died in infancy) - and in due course their eldest son, also called Walter, went to work at the Brewery with his father.

Walter junior married Kattie Cooke in 1890, set up house at Pondhu on the western side of the town and began to raise a family. Within two years, however, he moved back into the Brewery House when his father bought the lease of one of St Austell's grandest Victorian villas: The Brake, near Trenance.

Meanwhile there were even greater changes afoot as father and son set about finding a site for their new brewery. In 1893 they found the perfect place: two open fields off Tregonissey Lane (now called Trevarthian Road), on high ground with a dramatic view over the town and beyond to the arc of empty cliffs and sparkling sea in St Austell Bay. This was still countryside in the 1890s, well outside the limits of the town; the lane led from St Austell Church up past the steam brewery and the station above it, before heading into open country on the way to the village of Tregonissey. The two fields belonged, like so much land and property in the area, to the Sawle family of Penrice. On June 20th 1893 Walter was granted a 99-year improvement lease (the signatures witnessed, rather grandly, by *Henry Wenman, Butler to Sir Charles Brune Graves Sawle*).That original plot on which the

brewery was built measured just *two acres and three roods or thereabouts*; growth and new building in the last hundred years has seen the brewery site expand to some fourteen acres today.

A mere three days after the lease was signed, the *St Austell Star* reported that *'Mr Walter Hicks, of the St Austell Brewery, has accepted the tender of Messrs A.R. Lethbridge and Son, of Tracey Building Yard, Plymouth, for the erection of a new brewery. Messrs Inskipp and Mackenzie, of London, are the architects, and the amount of tender is between £7000 and £8000. Operations will be commenced on Monday next, and the building is to be completed in twelve months.'*

In the mid-nineteenth century there developed a new breed of architects and engineers who specialised in the construction and fitting out of breweries. The complexities of a brewery's physical requirements demanded a concentration of expertise not usually to be found in general architectural practices. The basic challenge was how to heat, cool, move and store huge volumes of liquid in an environment where ventilation and temperature could be controlled. The key, simply in terms of the building, was to take maximum advantage of gravity and the logical way to do this, particularly in smaller breweries, was to use the traditional tower system. This was basically a refined descendent of the domestic country-house brewhouse, but on an industrial scale. At its simplest, this system has the

OPPOSITE: *The new brewery, late 1890s.* ABOVE: *Walter Hicks junior with his daughter Corona.*

11

various stages of the brewing process taking place on descending levels within the tallest part of a brewery, beginning with the initial ingredients being pumped or hoisted to the top floor and ending with a perfect pint of beer at the bottom.

By the 1870s the practice of Davison, Inskipp and Mackenzie, established thirty years earlier by Robert Davison (described by Lynn Pearson as the father of brewery architects), had grown to become one of the top three specialist firms in the country. It is indicative of Walter Hicks's determination to get the best of everything that he commissioned this practice, by now called Inskipp and Mackenzie, to design his new brewery in 1893. In that same decade Inskipp and Mackenzie designed additions to some of the country's most famous breweries, including Courage's Anchor Brewery and Taylor Walker's Barley Mow Brewery in London.

Unlike some contemporaries, their work was known for being more functional than decorative. However, even the plainest Victorian industrial building has a grandeur and assurance that makes it stand out from the crowd. The most decorative and distinctive element of St Austell Brewery is the tall brick tower, a landmark for miles around, but it was not part of Inskipp and Mackenzie's design and not added until the early years of the twentieth century. Their original 1893 building, which is still the working heart of the brewery today, is an altogether more sober affair (if such an expression can be used about a brewery). It was built to work and built to last, of good materials and a robust construction, but still it has an unmistakable sense of style - a kind of austere splendour as befits its prominent position riding high on the St Austell skyline.

Walter senior had retired from the day-to-day running of the business in 1890, at the age of 61, but he continued to take an

TOP RIGHT: *The Brake in 1913.* RIGHT: *Caroline in the conservatory with two of her daughters.* FAR RIGHT CENTRE: *Hester and Elizabeth Barnes, Walter's grand-daughters, with the cockatoo, 1913.* FAR RIGHT: *An advertisement for Llewellins & James of Bristol,* c.1880s.

Life at The Brake

The Brake strikes an assured pose high on the precipitously steep western side of the Bodmin or Trenance valley, just over the brow of the hill from Trenance Farm. Far below, the main road to Bodmin runs alongside the St Austell River which rushes through dark overhanging woods and tangles of feral rhododendron. The Brake was built in the 1860s by Thomas Martin, one of the pioneers of the china clay industry, but it had been empty for some time before Walter bought it. On the steep slopes from the house down to the river the woods were cleared to make room for the formal terraced gardens which were carved into the hillside.

Canon Hammond, in *A Cornish Parish: an account of St Austell* published in 1897, writes of The Brake that *'it is the residence of Mr Walter Hicks, and is a conspicuous object from the railway bridge as the train passes over it. Two seafaring men were one day heard to observe that "a chap*

with that place and three or fower pounds a week could make hisself very comfortable"!' Having literally started on borrowed money just a few decades before, by the end of the century Walter was an extremely rich man by the standards of the day, and there is no doubt that life at The Brake was indeed comfortable if not verging on the opulent.

Walter junior's daughter Stella, who was born in 1896, has left us with the most vivid portrait of life at her grandparents' house at the turn of the century:

'I remember Granny [Caroline] as always wearing black silky dresses and lace caps with ribbons. I would sit on a footstool and she would teach me to sew. She was waited on hand and foot by her daughters - there would have been five of them at home at that time. I would be taken in to see her in the mornings before she was up and sit on her bed and recite the latest nursery rhyme I had learnt. After breakfast the servants would come in and join the family for prayers.

'The Brake was very attractive in those days. Looking across the valley to the Bodmin Road, the only building to be seen was the old toll cottage under the viaduct and no railway siding and houses as now. From the top of the garden one could sit and look down on a few cottages in Trenance Valley, and beyond nothing but fields and Pentewan Valley running down to the sea in the distance. Aunt Madge remembered being there when stone piers were being built on the railway viaduct to replace the old wooden ones, and saw a poor man fall to his death in the valley below. Fields on the slopes, and at the bottom of the grounds cows were kept to provide milk, cream and butter for the house.

'There was a long drive through the woods and up to the house from the Bodmin Road and a tennis court at the entrance. As it was always in the shade, no grass and I imagine the surface must have been gravel! I remember the family playing 'Bumble Puppy' - a tall pole with a tennis ball attached to a long cord from the top fret and played by two people with tennis racquets. Half way up the drive, a fountain playing and goldfish in a pond. At the front door, answered of course by a parlour maid with cap streamers, one went through the conservatory - oh that lovely warm earthy smell coming up through the gratings from the stoked furnace below, and the cockatoo screeching a greeting!'

active role in overseeing its development. From 1879 annual Brewers' Exhibitions - national showcases for architects, inventors and engineers - were held, initially in the Agricultural Hall in Islington, and it is not hard to imagine Walter Hicks setting off from St Austell station in his top hat to travel to London and immerse himself in all that was new in brewing. It would have been here that he discovered the work of Inskipp and Mackenzie, and specialist plant manufacturers and engineers such as George Adlam and Sons and Llewellins and James, both from Bristol. As with his first venture, this new brewery was to be fitted out with the latest and the best in brewing technology.

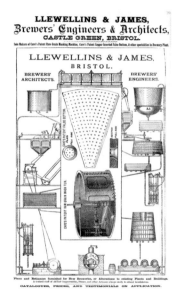

From Adlams, Walter bought a belt-driven malt grinding mill that is still in use at the brewery today. It was built in 1890, so if Walter bought it new then it would have started its working life down at the old brewery on Market Street before being moved up to the new site. Almost all of the original brewery plant has been modernised and replaced in the years since then, but this beautiful machine of polished wood and brass still does the job it was built for, rumbling and shaking like an old fairground ride on the top floor of the brewery tower.

One of the original slate fermenting vessels, made by *'Ernest Mathews & Co., Slate Back Manufacturers of London and Bristol'* probably dates from these early days. The older of the two mash tuns still in use today, made by Llewellins and James, was once thought to be of this date but is now considered to have been installed when the Brewery was enlarged in 1914. The one remaining small (40-barrel) steam-heated copper is, however, part of the original Brewery plant.

Whilst there had been all this growth and change at the core of his business, what of Walter Hicks's larger estate? As we have seen, Walter bought the leasehold of the Seven Stars at the bottom of East Hill in St Austell as early as 1863, and by 1893 he had bought a further eighteen pubs and hotels as far afield as Tavistock to the east and Gwennap to the west, closing down their brewhouses as he went. The prices of these establishments varied widely, no doubt reflecting their relative stature and condition; the Lanivet Inn was just £400 in 1893, whereas the Duke of Cornwall in Mount Charles, a large and important inn on the main road into St Austell from the east, had cost Walter £2800 four years earlier. By 1910 the Brewery's estate had grown to 54 pubs and hotels and several more leaseholds and yearly tenancies, plus stores to aid distribution in Plymouth, Truro, St Blazey, Camborne and Penzance.

There were far fewer public houses in Cornwall by the end of the century than there had been when Walter was starting out in business, and they were mostly better regulated and run. The number of on-licences in the county dropped from 1,036 in 1864 to 650 in 1889, due to a number of factors of which the pressure of Methodism and the temperance movement was one and the shifting and loss of the mining industry another. However, the licensing authorities still had their fair share of trouble with disreputable beer shops and local dens of iniquity, and even the *bona fide* hotels and inns which catered for travellers sometimes had less than salubrious reputations. The *Royal Cornwall Gazette* in 1892 reported that two-thirds of the county's convictions for drunkenness had occurred in the parish of St Austell. The Chairman of the Annual Licensing Sessions remarked that *'It was an extraordinary thing where the*

RIGHT: *The Commercial Inn, St Dennis, 1856.* FAR RIGHT: *Great Western Railway at Penzance, 1904.*

Cornish pubs in 1852

The Victorian novelist Wilkie Collins travelled through Cornwall on a walking holiday, and in his endlessly delightful account of this journey - *Rambles Beyond Railways* - describes some of the inns he encountered.

In Saltash, for instance: '*There was no mistaking the tavern. The only light on shore gleamed from the tavern window; and, judging by the criterion of noise, the whole local population seemed to be collected within the tavern walls. We opened the door; and found ourselves in a small room, filled with shrimpers, sailors, fishermen and watermen, all "looming large" through a fog of tobacco, and all chirping merrily over their cups; while the hostess sat apart on a raised seat in a corner, calm and superior amidst the hubbub...*'

And in Morvah in the far west: '*...fancy the largest of the buildings being called an inn, but making up no beds, because nobody ever stopped to sleep there: fancy in the kitchen of this inn a sickly little girl, and a middle-aged melancholy woman, the first staring despondingly on a wasting fire, the second setting before the stranger a piece of bread, three eggs, and some sour porter, corked down in an earthenware jar, as all that her larder and cellar afforded...*'

And again in Liskeard: '*Not a human being appeared in the street where this tavern of despair frowned amid congenial desolation! Nobody welcomed us at the door - the sign creaked dolefully, as the wind swung it on its rusty hinges. We walked in; and discovered a little man sitting at an empty "bar", and hiding himself, as it were, from all mortal inspection behind the full sheet of a dirty provincial newspaper...Food there was none in the house, saving a piece of corned beef, which the family had dined on, and which he proposed that we should partake of before it got quite cold. Having said thus much, he suddenly retired behind his newspaper, and spoke no word more.*'

THE ERECTION OF THE
ALBERT
RIDGE SALTASH 1857

*people got drunk. He did not think the peculiar air of St Austell was
of such a high alcoholic character as to account for it. They must
have got drunk in Public Houses and he only wished it could be
brought home to someone. He had private information that at the
Miners Inn, Nanpean, and the Mount Charles Inn, St Austell, a
great deal of drinking took place and that they wanted a good deal
of looking after. As far as he was concerned he would not renew the
licences of these two houses.'*

Way above all other influences, however, the extension of the
national railway network to Cornwall, through the engineering
skills and efforts of Isambard Kingdom Brunel, was to bring about
a gradual but ultimately fundamental change in the nature of the
county's pubs and hotels, and was moreover to have a profound
effect upon the future prosperity of Walter Hicks's Brewery. The
opening of the Royal Albert Bridge over the Tamar at Saltash in
1859 heralded the era of mass tourism. It was only a trickle at first,
and its true power and consequence was not to be felt until the
following century, but already by the 1890s it was clear to anyone
with ambitions in the victualling or hospitality business that the
requirements of Cornwall's visitors needed to be addressed.

ABOVE: *Building the Royal Albert Bridge.* RIGHT: *The Brake spring.*
FAR RIGHT: *Walter Hicks in 1914.*

The vital source

*'Water being one of the essential materials used in brewing, it is necessary that every brewery
and malting should have an abundant and constant supply. In fixing upon the site of a brewery, it
is a matter of great importance that the water used for brewing should be of a kind to produce
the article that is required.'* (The Brewing Industry by Julian L. Baker, 1905).

Back in 1886 Walter Hicks sent a sample of Town Water for analysis to a London firm of
analytical chemists. Their report concluded that whilst it was *'a first rate town supply...for
brewing purposes it is naturally not so well adapted seeing that it lacks the saline constituents so
essential to the production of high class pale and bitter ales.'* They recommended that it
should be artificially hardened through the addition of Burton Water Crystals which *'would
bring it up very closely indeed to the Burton standard of excellence'* (the water of Burton-on-
Trent being so suited to the production of light ales that it had become a national
benchmark), but that for the brewing of stout and porter it was perfectly constituted and
needed no additives.

We do not know if Walter took their advice or used a private well when brewing in the
town, but once he had chosen the site for his new brewery he saw it as a priority to locate
an independent and reliable source of water for brewing. He found it two miles up the
Bodmin valley at Ruddlemoor, again on land belonging to Sir Charles Graves Sawle who
granted him the *'liberty, license and authority to take, use and divert...the springs and streams of
water arising in or flowing from the lands...being part of the Estate of Ruddle'*, and to lay a
pipeline all the way down the valley and up over the fields of Menacuddle Farm behind the
Brewery. The source was only eighteen inches higher than the brewery site but that was
enough to enable the water to flow by gravity without the need for pumps.

In 1906 a superior source of fresh water was found close by, issuing from an old adit
(horizontal mine tunnel) on land belonging to the Martyn family of Carthew, which is now
part of the Wheal Martyn China Clay Museum. A new lease was signed and the pipe was
extended a few hundred yards further up the valley to the adit mouth. The Carthew adit
remained the Brewery's primary water supply until about thirty years ago, when the
expansion and deepening of a china clay pit just over the hill interrupted the supply and it
began to dry up. This could have been a disaster, but since 1912 there had been a second
source of water to help fill the reservoirs behind the Brewery. This spring, known at first as
The Polkeys but now called The Brake from its position in the valley bottom immediately
below Walter's old house (close to Menacuddle Well), now provides all the brewing water
('liquor'). Its origins are mysterious: it rises in a narrow cavern, thought to be an old mine
working, which runs deep into the hillside below the Bodmin Road. A limpid pool of
unknown depth and constant purity, its level only dropped six inches during the drought of
1976. Modern pumps propel the water up the hill to the Brewery, and a recent development

now has the waste water being returned to the river, after purification, just a few feet downstream from The Brake spring.

There is one more source of water used by the Brewery: the 'deep well' in the original cooper's shop which is said to have been dug by out of work miners early in the twentieth century. The particularly pure water in this well is used for general purposes today - cask washing and so forth - but in the 1920s it was also being used for brewing.

In 1910 Walter and his son took the decision to register their business as a limited company. The Memorandum of Association lists a bewildering number of *'objects for which the Company is established'*, over and above the core concerns of brewing and wine and spirit merchants, including: *'any or all of the businesses of hop-merchants and growers, maltsters, maltfactors and corn merchants, bonded store keepers, wine and spirit importers and distillers, coopers and bottlers, bottlemakers, bottle stop makers, case makers, potters, manufacturers of and dealers in aerated and mineral waters and other drinks, licensed victuallers, hotel-keepers, beerhouse keepers, restaurant keepers, lodging-house keepers, ice manufacturers and merchants, tobacconists, farmers, dairy-men, yeast dealers, grain sellers and driers, timber merchants, brick makers, finings manufacturers, isinglass merchants, miners and producers and merchants of china clay and china stone'.*

At the first AGM of *'Walter Hicks & Company Ltd'* held on 6th April 1910, Walter Hicks senior was appointed Governing Director and a share capital of 10,000 shares was divided between himself and his ten children. The business was prosperous and stable; all seemed to augur well for the new company.

What should have been a comfortable and untroubled old age for Walter was, however, to be shattered just a year later. Walter junior shared his father's love of new machines and had bought his first motor cycle as early as 1904 (a 3hp Rover, registered AF145). Thereafter he had a succession of these pioneering vehicles; they were his preferred mode of transport as he travelled around the county seeing to the Brewery's scattered estate. On the morning of 20th April 1911 he was riding down through Helston when he collided with a motor car travelling in the opposite direction and was thrown backwards off the motor cycle onto the road, fracturing his skull. The *Cornish Guardian* reported that the three gentlemen in the car *'placed Mr Hicks, who was unconscious, in their car and drove to Dr Anderson's surgery. Unfortunately there was no medical man in the town at the time, and the sufferer was then carried to a chemist's shop where first aid was rendered by PC Clarke...At first Mr Hicks was in a precarious condition, but he has since rallied somewhat and hopes are entertained for his recovery.'* The report concluded with the news that *'the eminent London specialist Sir Victor Horsley pronounced that he would recover consciousness in a few days.'* Tragically, this was not to be the case and Walter died one week later. On the day of his funeral, *'one of the largest ever witnessed in the town'*, the *St Austell Star* described how *'about fifty employees of the St Austell Brewery preceded the hearse, and at the church gates formed a body guard. The Brewery was closed all day and business in the town was practically suspended during the internment.'*

What a devastating blow this must have been for old Walter. Quite apart from the grief of a father losing his son, there was his business to think about. He had sought to found not just a company but a dynasty, and now at the age of 82 he must have seen all that he had created suddenly look shaky and impermanent. The provision of a secure male line to carry on the

RIGHT: *Screen in Luxulyan Church erected by Walter Hicks as a memorial to his son.*
FAR RIGHT: *Walter and Hester in the garden of The Brake.*

Family and community

In 1910 Walter Hicks was 81 years old; a venerable and impressive figure in family photographs, with his snowy white beard and stern countenance. He lived the life of an Edwardian gentleman, cared for by his unmarried daughters after Caroline died in 1901. His and his family's position in society and material wealth had been founded purely upon his own ambition, business acumen and determination to succeed.

On the St Austell social scene, Walter had been rubbing shoulders with local landowners and the china clay 'aristocracy' since the 1870s. A.L. Rowse's description of those men whose fortune and public standing came from clay has a familiar ring to it, for it could just as well describe the founder of the Brewery: *'This was the halcyon time when the entrenched clay families made their money, heaps of it - at any rate a great deal for small people in a small place. This was the time when their villas burgeoned on the western outskirts of the town, when they prudently - they were never spendthrift - bought their first motor-cars'.*

These were the men who ran St Austell, a town which had grown so rapidly in the second half of the nineteenth century, and helped to give it its civic structure. Before the advent of town and parish councils, the St Austell District Local Board governed the affairs of the town, employed the fire brigade and was generally responsible for town planning and improvements such as sewerage and lighting. Walter was already a member in 1869, when he was elected to serve as overseer of the parish, and by 1889 he was its Chairman. *'At a recent festive board,'* the *St Austell Star* reported in 1893, *'Mr Hicks humorously referred to his trade as a "poor downtrodden one" at which everybody had a kick. The "mayor" of St Austell is not without his humorous moods. This must have been one of them'.* Along with other prominent citizens, Walter was also a long-standing officer with the local Peace and Harmony Lodge of Freemasonry.

The entire Hicks family was deeply involved with the life of the parish church; Walter junior, in particular, served as churchwarden, sidesman and bellringer (he was Captain of the Tower for nearly 25 years). His daughter Stella remembered Canon Hammond being a frequent visitor to the old Brewery House, where they lived until moving up the hill to Tregarne House in 1902, and vividly recalled the recasting of the church's *'fine peal of eight bells'* which her father so loved to ring: *'It was fascinating living so near to watch them being brought through a window in the tower and lowered to the ground, and the same in reverse when they came back. How our local fire brigade managed while they were being recast I don't know, as the big deep toned bell was used to summon them when there was a fire. It sent shivers down one's spine to be woken up at night by the sound of its quick clang clang.'*

The funeral of Walter Hicks junior

'While the muffled bells of St Austell Church tolled a solemn peal and crowds of mournful spectators with sorrowful hearts lined the streets, the body of Mr Walter Hicks junior was borne to its final resting place at St Austell Cemetery on Monday morning. The tragic death of one so universally respected lent a mournful interest to the internment, and seldom has St Austell paid such heartfelt tribute to one of its departed sons. It was an hour of general sorrow locally, and all classes alike gathered to pay their last respects to a townsman... Business houses were partially closed, and not a window was there along the entire route that was not curtained as a token of esteem and sympathy with the bereaved family.' The *Cornish Guardian*, 5th May 1911.

business and the family name was absolutely crucial. He had ten children, but only two were sons and now one of them, his eldest, his heir and his successor in the Brewery, was dead. His other son, George, had no interest in following his brother into the family firm. He had eight grandchildren, but again only two of them were boys and before he died he was to lose one of them, the only grandson who bore his name, in the war: Gerald Hicks, Walter junior's son, was killed at Armentières in 1915. Gerald was shot by a German sniper during a scouting mission. He was 21, and news of his promotion to Lieutenant came through shortly after his death. His Colonel wrote: *'He was one of the most gallant boys I have ever met and would go anywhere and do anything. His men adored him and his Captain could not speak too highly of him. He was intensely gallant and did not know the word "fear".'* A brother officer wrote simply: *'His men worshipped him and no words of mine can describe to you what he did for them.'*

It might have looked disastrous at the time, but with hindsight we know that Walter's dynasty did not let him down. Quite unexpectedly, it was in his remarkable eldest daughter that Walter found a worthy heir who went on to do him and his Brewery proud.

The Ship Inn, Mousehole

In 1901 the Ship in Mousehole became the Brewery's most distant public house when it was bought for £900. This traditional eighteenth-century pub overlooking the harbour still has its floors of scrubbed wood and huge granite flags, snugs and stained glass, low black beams and burnished panelling; its unforced charm has survived because it has been left alone. The parlour was painted by the famous Newlyn artist Stanhope Forbes (*The Green Mantleshelf*, later exhibited at the Royal Academy), and if he were to walk in there again today he would find that little had changed. The Ship was also a favoured haunt of the poet Dylan Thomas when he lived in Mousehole up on steep Raginnis Hill ('*Raginnis-is-good-for-you Hill*' as he called it) in the 1930s, but today it is best known as the home of Star-gazey Pie and as the hub of festivities on Tom Bawcock's Eve.

The Ship Inn, Fowey

Walter Hicks bought the leasehold of the Ship for £500 in 1891. One of Fowey's oldest buildings, it had been the town house of the Rashleigh family. It was known as 'the Ship House' long before it became an inn because of a model of John Rashleigh's famous Elizabethan ship the *Francis* (complete with anchors, rigging, guns and men) which used to hang above the doorway on an iron chain. It is not known when the Ship ceased to be a private house, but as long ago as 1758 it was said that *'It hath been an inn of the chiefest note, in the place where situate, for a long series of time.'* A striking remnant of the old house is an oak panelled room, now a guest bedroom, carved with the figure of Elizabeth I and the date 1570.

The heroic exploits of John Rashleigh are recalled in a Victorian stained-glass window in the dining room (originally from the Old Vicarage, it was bought for the Ship in 1966) depicting *'Ye Shippes of Fowey Haven preparing to welcome ye Armada'*.

Rashleigh and his ship are also depicted in the dramatic scenes painted on two exterior walls in 1947 by the celebrated muralist Hans Feibusch. A German Jew who had lived in England since 1933, Feibusch is known particularly for his many church murals, and for his classical subjects painted for Clough Williams-Ellis at Portmeirion in Wales.

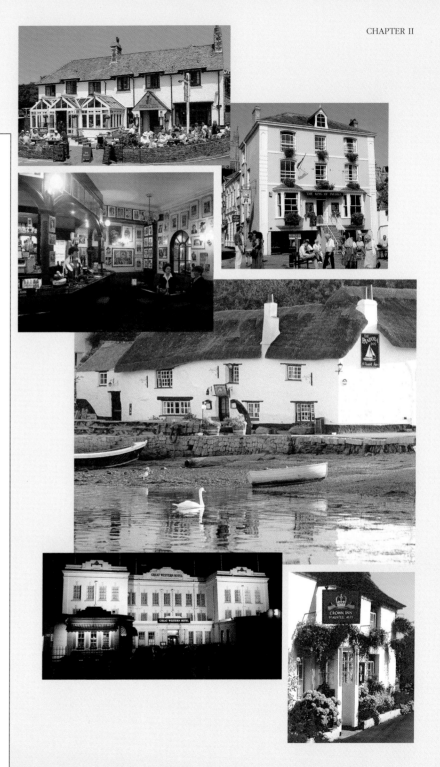

FAR LEFT: *from top to bottom: Victoria Stores, Newquay, 1936; the White Hart, St Austell, 1909; Mrs. and Miss Barron of the Ship Inn, Mevagissey, 1936; Mr. W. Bennetts of the Queens Head, St Stephen, 1936; the Prince of Wales, Devonport, 1936; the Central Inn, Newquay, 1936.* LEFT: *the Ship Inn, Mousehole.* BACKGROUND: *Mousehole, 1938.* ABOVE: *Hans Feibusch mural on the Ship Inn, Fowey.* RIGHT: *from top to bottom: the Rising Sun, St Mawes; the King of Prussia, Fowey; the bar of the White Hart; the Pandora Inn, Restronguet; the Great Western Hotel, Newquay; the Crown Inn, St Ewe.*

21

THIS PAGE: *Hester Parnall.* OPPOSITE: *Walter Hicks and Tom Parnall* c.*1914*

CHAPTER III

A woman's touch

Immediately after his son's death, the 82-year-old Walter Hicks returned to take the helm at the Brewery, but not for long. The minutes of the directors' meeting on 22nd May 1911 read: *'I Walter Hicks do hereby appoint Hester Parnall, wife of Thomas Parnall of Belfield, St Austell, to be a Director of this Company in the place of Walter Hicks jnr now deceased'.* We can only imagine that Walter was astute enough to recognise in his daughter the qualities needed to run a business, and not to be put off by the many disadvantages of being a woman in small-town Edwardian Cornwall. The Suffragette Movement might have been making the headlines in London, but its effects were barely felt in St Austell. Even today Hester would be seen as an unusually impressive figure in the business world; back then she must have been extraordinary.

Hester Parnall was 45 years old when her brother died. She had remained at home at The Brake, as one of Walter's large clutch of unmarried daughters, until the age of 39 when she married Thomas Parnall and went to live with him in some grandeur at Belfield on the Truro Road (now a residential home called Gwethnoc Parc). 'Uncle Tom' was 27 years her senior; he was a kind and artistic man, an accomplished painter who loved the outdoor life and is remembered with great affection by those who knew him. Marriage to Tom gave Hester the status which her spinster sisters, however accomplished they might have been, never achieved; you would always be taken more seriously as a Mrs than a Miss.

Hester's niece Stella remembered her as a woman of strong character: *'I have heard her described as clever, witty and utterly unscrupulous. I think this last description is somewhat unfair, but one had to remember that the Aunts led very restricted lives in a small country town where there was little opportunity of fulfilling any ambition and meeting new people, or hopes of marriage or travel.'* Significantly for the future of the Brewery, Stella's son Tim Harvey considers that Hester *'had many of the characteristics and qualities of my great-grandfather',* (whom he imagines was *'rumbustious and domineering, autocratic and impressive'*) which young Walter, *'a much quieter, gentler sort of person',* did not possess. Clifford Hockin, who started as an office boy in the Brewery in 1926 before progressing to Company Secretary in 1963, memorably described her as *'ruling the Company with the grace of a duchess combined with the aplomb of the successful business man'.*

Hester had just five years in which to learn all that her father knew about running the Brewery. It was during this period that the brewhouse underwent some major changes to increase production. Walter Hicks's new brewery in 1893 had roughly double the capacity of his first brewery in the town; now alterations, new building and new plant installed between 1912 and 1914 doubled the capacity again, so that in less than 50 years Walter quadrupled his potential output. An extra copper room was built to house a new 100-barrel copper, replacing one of the original 40-barrel coppers,

and a new enlarged fermenting room was added. However, before the work was finished the war had broken out and the effect of the consequent restricted output, escalating beer duties, reduction in beer strengths and quality, and a shortage of men and raw materials, was that this new capacity was not exploited until after 1918. By the '20s the output was close to 38,000 barrels per annum, around twice what it had been before the war.

Walter Hicks died on 4th April 1916 at the age of 87. In reporting the news of his death, the *Cornish Guardian* commented that *'a familiar figure passes out of the commercial life of the town... Mr Hicks took an active interest in the business, which under his guidance grew to such large dimensions, up to his death. He enjoyed a splendid constitution, and was in possession of all his faculties to the last. It was not until Sunday that he became seriously ill.'* Hester was made Chairman of the company on the death of her father, and under the terms of his Will she was joined on the board by her brother-in-law Reginald Garrould Barnes.

R.G. Barnes, who had married Hester's sister Mary in 1896, was the Brewery's London solicitor. He was to be a constant support to Hester in her new role, and her letters make it clear that as a matter of course she would seek his advice and respect his experience in the world of business. Her other steadfast ally was Alfred

ABOVE: *Reginald Barnes and Mary Hicks, at The Brake on their wedding day, 1896.*
RIGHT: *Extract from Walter's Executorship and Distribution Accounts.*
FAR RIGHT: *Hester (left) in 1922.*

Extracts from Walter's will

'I bequeath all my plate and plated articles, furniture, linen, glass, china, pictures, prints, musical instruments, books...and also all my horses and carriages with their harness apparel and furniture, my motor cars with their accessories, my cows and other live and dead stock, my hothouse and greenhouse plants and other plants in pots and my stable and garden implements (but not including my small motor car nor any live or dead stock, carts, carriages, harness, implements or other chattels which at the time of my death may be used for the purpose of any trade or business in which I may be interested) unto such one or more of my daughters (except my daughter Margaret) as at my death shall not have been married...'. His unfortunate daughter Margaret *'for whom I have already otherwise provided'* was excluded from all bequests in his Will following a distressing family scandal in 1909. Poor Margaret became pregnant as a result of a love affair with a married vicar, a shattering event in those days, and was banished to Bournemouth where her child died at birth. Walter never saw her again and, as Stella later put it, *'cut her off with the proverbial shilling, though in this case it was £18,000 which was very securely tied up.'* Thereafter she lived so frugally that when she died in 1957 at the age of 84, £10,000 of interest, in addition to the original sum, was returned to her family.

Walter left Lower Menadue to his son George, but it continued to be farmed by tenants as George lived and farmed at Menacuddle just behind the Brewery. To his son-in-law R.G. Barnes, in addition to a directorship and shares in the company, he left *'my one-fourth part of or share in the business of Thomas Olver and Company China Stone Merchants'.* Hester and R.G. Barnes were appointed his Executors, and Trustees for the residue of his estate.

Memories of Hester Parnall

Clifford Hockin (worked at the Brewery 1926-1975): *'Although Hester usually visited the Brewery each morning around 11am, it was never taken for granted. All who came in contact with her, and indeed those who did not, were on their best behaviour. Before the day-to-day business was discussed, her pair of Pekingese dogs were carefully sited on the desk in the Board Room on pieces of white blotting paper laid out by the office boy [Clifford himself].'*

Tom Stephens (worked at the Brewery 1924-1973): *'The first man to spot her chauffeur-driven Daimler arriving in the yard would tap out a message of warning on the water pipes which could be heard throughout the Brewery. She once sacked a chap she caught painting with a fag in his mouth, and she sacked one of the drivers for picking up a passenger; she was a proper dragon!'*

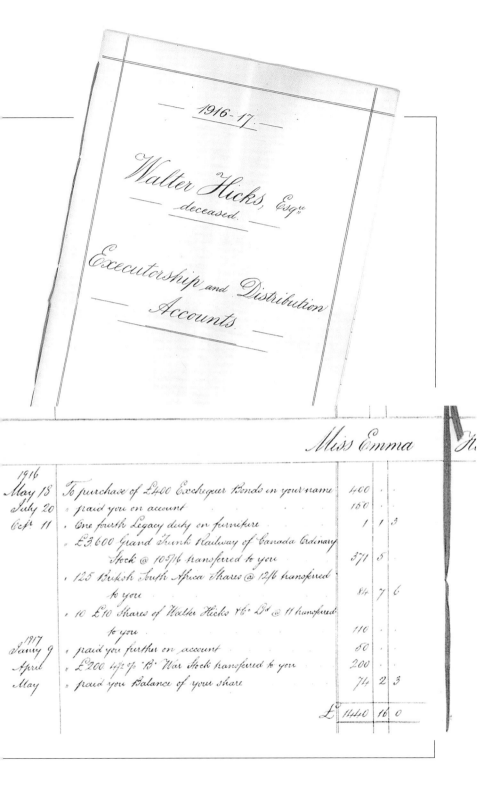

Ashton who had worked for the Brewery since 1901 and whom she made the first Manager and Secretary of the company in 1916. Their relationship was formal, as you would expect from their relative positions and the era in which they worked, but their correspondence during the times when Hester was absent from the Brewery suggests that it was also invested with mutual respect and a genuine warmth. *It is very comforting to me to know that things are going smoothly under your direction'*, she wrote to Ashton in 1924, *'and on that score I have no anxiety.'*

Despite the abilities of these two men, and the invaluable experience of brewery workers such as Mr Smallwood who took over from Mr Biscoe as Head Brewer in 1912, there is no doubt that Hester Parnall was a hands-on Chairman who involved herself with all the day-to-day aspects of running the business. Her husband Tom had died in 1915, so after her father's death the following year she moved into The Brake. In the early 1920s, however, she spent much of her time in London (before returning to Cornwall to live at Tregrehan in 1927) and a mass of correspondence between Hester and Alfred Ashton during this period has survived. Thanks to the efficiency and speed of the postal and telegram services in those days, sometimes as many as three missives a day went winging their way between London and St Austell, dealing with everything from transport and brewing plant to individual workers' problems and the price of hops. These letters demonstrate Hester's demand for - and her grasp of - the details of the business at every step, as well as a financial caution that verges on meanness (contrasting, we are told, with the extravagance of her private life!). They also reveal her sharp mind, her wit, and her tendency to be forthright, opinionated and above all decisive on any matter (one memorable telegram in 1925 simply reads *'Yes. Parnall.'*).

Hester, with Barnes and Ashton, guided the Brewery astutely through the difficult post-war years which culminated in the economic depression of the 1930s, and under her chairmanship the company grew rapidly. The Brewery workforce expanded from 62 in 1910 to more than 80 before the outbreak of the Second World War, and in her 23 years at the helm she oversaw the acquisition of an astonishing 79 pubs and hotels.

ABOVE: *Early Walter Hicks bottles.* RIGHT: *Arthur Dumble and Tom Searley in the cask yard, 1942 (40 years' and 51 years' service respectively).* FAR RIGHT: *Brewery stables, 1890s.*

Hester's letters

12th September 1925, Alfred Ashton to Hester Parnall: *'I regret to inform you that burglars broke into our Offices last night through one of the side windows between the Offices and the Bottling Store. They did not attempt to touch the Safes but forced the whole of the drawers in the three bottom offices that were locked. Their total haul was about £6 which is Petty Cash received for small sales of Tobacco etc....It is the first time that a burglary has been committed here since I came 25 years ago.'*

1st January 1924, Alfred Ashton to Hester Parnall: *'Enclosed I hand you particulars of a new Foden Wagon which Jenkins of Watering is offering for £550, the price of which today is £835. Our Foden is getting pretty well worn out and I do not know what your intentions are about replacing it, so I simply enclose this letter for your consideration.'*

3rd January, Alfred Ashton to Hester Parnall: *'On receipt of your telephone message today about the Foden Wagon, I saw the driver of our present Foden who told me that the one we have will go on for a year or two with little repairs...'*

5th January, Hester Parnall to Alfred Ashton: *'...it would be needless extravagance to buy another, especially as the work is almost exclusively station work; prices of machines are steadily dropping, and when we really need one, I daresay there will be one available.'*

Brewery memories

Tom Stephens ('Tom Pip') started in the unloading shed and the wash-house in 1924, earning a 'boy's wage' of 7/6 a week, before moving to the bottling store and then to the Pop Shop, where he was paid a man's wage of £3. For three months of the year he did not get home at night until 11 or midnight, and had to be in again at 7. He had been keen to work up at the Brewery because all his friends were there, but when a vacancy came up it caused much concern to his mother and father, who were strict Wesleyans: *'They had the minister come over and they spent hours saying their prayers as to whether it was right for me to go to work at such a place of temptation. Part of the job was learning how to drink, but my excuse to mother when I got home the worse for wear was that the fumes in the Brewery had made me drunk.'*

Jack Dumble, who worked at the Brewery for 33 years, alongside his father and two of his brothers, remembered being called to be a referee at a drinking contest between Tom Searley and Arnold Walkey, at 6.45 in the morning: *'They had three gallon buckets full of beer, and Arnold did it in six minutes, on his knees like a horse.'*

Inevitably, with this huge expansion in the Brewery's estate throughout the county, the question of distribution became a priority. Until the 1920s, properties within a twelve-mile radius of the Brewery were supplied by horse and dray, with the railway system - then much more extensive than today - used for places further afield. In this predominantly rural county, scattered settlements and population rather than a concentrated urban base provided the Brewery's economic foundation, so horses had a crucial role to play in its early development. An L-shaped stable block closed the brewery yard to the south and east, and occupying pride of place in the middle of the yard was an enormous manure heap. Up to 20 horses lived here at any one time, their names recorded in old account books - Polly, Harold, Lion, Madam, Joey, Beauty, Kicker, Prince - and their hay, straw and mangolds supplied from Lower Menadue and Menacuddle Farms.

The Guinness Brewery in Dublin had tried out the first steam wagons in 1897; true to form Walter Hicks was not far behind and as early as 1906 there was a steam Foden and a steam Straker covering the short run between the Brewery and St Austell Goods Station, just down the hill. In 1912 they were joined by another Foden, and during the First World War they

The Brewery staff in 1925. *This photograph, taken at the same time as the one of the transport fleet on p30, was the subject of an amusing discourse between Alfred Ashton and Hester Parnall in which her parsimony and his gentle insistence are well illustrated...*

AA to HP: 'I enclose herewith photographs of the Waggons and Staff at the Brewery. The largest of the Staff are 5/-, the next size 3/6 and the small size 2/- each. I think they are splendid and should be pleased to hear what you think about them.'

HP to AA: 'I think the photographs are excellent. Of the staff photographs I should order three at 5/-, twelve at 3/6 and as many of the small size to give one each to the staff (excepting the Clerical Staff who will have those at 3/6).'

AA to HP: 'I have made enquiries and find that everyone without exception is anxious to have a 5/- or a 3/6 size as they do not care for the small ones. They are quite agreeable to pay the difference between the cost of the small one and the one they order...They appear to look at the group as being useful as a picture in their homes.'

Mentioned by name in the text: Alfred Ashton (bottom row 8 from left). G Smallwood (bottom row 7 from left). Bill Hockin (bottom row 2 from left). Tom Stephens (3rd row 3 from left). Tom Searley (3rd row 8 from left). Arnold Walkey (4th row 4 from left).

Brewery families

Throughout the history of St Austell Brewery, it is noticeable how the same names keep cropping up time and again from one generation to the next: names like Hancock, Stephens, Hockin, Wescott, Cocks, Little, Henwood, Poad, Allen, Herbert, Brewer, Dumble, Searley, Walkey, Monk and Sprague. This is a true family business not just in the traditional sense - in that Walter Hicks's descendents still own and run the company - but also in that successive generations of local families have been involved in all aspects of the Brewery's work, so that over the years a tradition of family loyalty and pride in the company has developed to strengthen its very fabric and foundation.

Tom Stephens was proud that his family could notch up more than 200 years of service to the Brewery, with a total of fourteen members of the family having worked there since he started in 1924. He remembered being so careful not to show favouritism to his son that *'I went too far the other way. He said I was the worst boss ever!'.*

RIGHT: *Award certificate 1914.* FAR RIGHT: *Brewery dray delivering in St Ives, 1900.*

Brewery memories

Clifford Hockin: *'Fred Burchall was the chief horse-man, a seven day week job, on call 24 hours a day. For this service he enjoyed rent-free accommodation of the cottage adjoining the stables. He lost this job and cottage when it became known that for two evenings a week he was running a Hoop-la Stall in the Market House. He then drove the steam Foden for a time but lost this job too as he never could stop the Foden without shouting 'Whoa! Whoa there!' in panic at the top of his voice.'*

In 1924 the Brewery bought a new boiler, the old one having been condemned by the Boiler Insurance Co., and Clifford Hockin remembers the Foden being used to haul it up the hill from the railway station: *'This was an exciting event and attracted much interest throughout the journey. The boiler was both loaded on to the new five-ton Leyland petrol lorry and on to the Foden to distribute the weight. The Foden was to lead and the Leyland to follow, but in reverse gear. All went well, very slowly, until the steep entrance to the Brewery was reached, when the front wheels of the Foden rose into the air like a prancing horse.'*

The following letter from Alfred Ashton to Hester Parnall makes it clear that the boiler completed its journey successfully, as well as revealing something of the fondness in their working relationship: *'I regret very much to hear that your are unwell and not able to come down. I shall feel quite lost without you at the Meeting tomorrow but after all I do not consider it wise for you to run any risks whatever. You can rest assured that all matters will be carried through in proper order by Mr Barnes and myself...I am pleased to say that everything is alright at the Brewery and the Fires of the New Boiler were lit by Miss Carrie* [Hester's sister Caroline Hicks] *and Mr Barnes this morning.'*

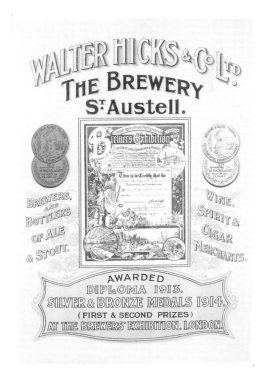

were used to deliver beer to the army camp on St Anthony Head at the entrance to Falmouth Harbour - a journey that took them two days. In 1928 the Great Western Railway offered to cart all goods between the Station and the Brewery at 2/6 per ton, but Hester considered that *'whilst the Foden is still running it is cheaper to cart ourselves.'* At that time the annual cost of running the Foden Steam Wagon was estimated as:

Wages 2 Men - £301.12.0   Coal - £93.12.0   Oil etc. - £20.16.0
Repairs, say - £12.0.0   Licence - £54.0.0   Insurance - £18.0.0
TOTAL - £500.0.0 per annum.

Before long the first petrol lorries joined the horses and the steamers - initially two Federals, two Maxwells and a Thornycroft - but the horses' days were numbered. The minutes of the directors' meeting on 3rd July 1923 recorded the resolution *'to purchase a two-ton and a five- or six-ton Leyland lorry. Horses to be disposed of as soon as big lorry is delivered'.* However, horses continued to be used elsewhere in the county to deliver from certain stations to the outlying pubs. Ashton

wrote to Hester Parnall in May 1925 that: *'Maunder has appealed to me for additional help for his delivery of goods at Newquay…The season is fast approaching and we have nothing there at present but a worn out old horse and wagon and every appearance of having a very busy time.'* In 1930 it was reported from Penzance *'that at the present we are hiring transport owing to the horse having died…'*

As the Brewery expanded its estate and updated its transport system, so much of Hester's and R.G. Barnes's attention was also given to modernising some of the brewing plant which new advances, particularly in bottling and refrigeration, had rendered obsolete. Crown corks, now the usual method of sealing bottles, were introduced during this period; an American invention patented in 1892, they revolutionised the production of bottled beers, in terms of both the speed of the bottling and the efficiency of the seal. The Brewery bought its first crown corking machine second-hand for £40 in 1927 from the Friary Brewery in Guildford.

The Lugger Inn, Polruan

This traditional quayside fisherman's pub had been owned and run by successive generations of the Hicks family (no relation, but a long-standing Polruan family) for nearly a century when it came up for auction in 1937. By this time, Hester's health was failing and her old allies Alfred Ashton and R.G. Barnes had both died. In Ashton's place as Manager and Secretary there was A.S.B. Payne, who had proved a worthy and dependable successor. Payne wrote to Hester in November 1937 that *'On Wednesday I went to Polruan to look at the Lugger Hotel. It is quite a nice little house and beautifully kept, but it is like all these old fashioned houses and has a lot of small rooms and not any large ones.'*

At the auction the Brewery was outbid by an individual who paid £4,415. It was, in Payne's view, *'an absurd price'*, but he was at least relieved that the pub had not been bought by a rival brewery such as Devenish or Redruth because he had established that the buyer would be likely to have the Brewery supply it as a free house. However, in the minutes of the Directors' Meeting held in January 1938 it was reported that *'the purchaser subsequently was unable to complete and offered the house to the Company and the property was purchased for £3,800 on January 5th'*.

ABOVE: *The transport fleet in 1925, housed in the old stables.* RIGHT: *Early Walter Hicks bottles, including Stonegingers, and Ellis Brewery labels.* FAR RIGHT: *Sketch by R. G. Barnes of possible crown cork design, included in letter - far right.*

The St Kew Inn

In 1922 Hester Parnall bought the St Kew Inn, today one of the Brewery's best-loved rural pubs, as one of eight properties owned by the business of A. Coombes & Son of Wadebridge. Coombes were described as *'Wine and Spirit Merchants, Mineral Water Manufacturer, Hop Merchant, Maltsters and Cigar Merchants'*, and for an outlay of just £6,500 the Brewery acquired some notable houses - including the Golden Lion in Port Isaac and the Earl of St Vincent in Egloshayle - along with the Eddystone Road headquarters of the business itself.

The beautifully-proportioned Georgian building, set close by the church in the classic Cornish churchtown of St Kew, started out as a private house but has been the St Kew Inn since the early nineteenth century. What is now the public bar was once the hall-kitchen of that house; the slate flagstones and black settles, the meat hooks hanging from the ceiling, and the vast fireplace with a cast-iron expanding grate and logs stacked on either side are reminders of the pub's former life.

Prior to this, the bottles were sealed with either corks (stoppers, as opposed to driven corks, at this stage), screws or 'cods'. The oldest cod bottles were pear-shaped and had a glass marble inside which, combined with a rubber ring at the mouth, acted as a seal when the bottles were filled under pressure. In its Mineral Waters department (the 'Pop Shop'), which had been an essential part of Walter Hicks's business from the earliest days, the Brewery produced prize-winning lemonade, ginger beer, mineral water and soda water. In the early days most of the minerals were bottled in cods, but soda water was also produced in syphons, whilst the celebrated Hicks's Ginger Beer came in half-pint corked and wired stone bottles known as 'Stonegingers'.

Two of the most significant changes in the Brewery's history came in 1934. In October, after lengthy and complex negotiations, the company bought Christopher Ellis & Son's Steam Brewery at Hayle, together with its estate of 30 licensed premises, for £50,000. In the same year the name of the company was changed to *'St Austell Brewery Co. Ltd'*. This was not such a surprising move as for many years it had been referred to as 'the St Austell Brewery' both informally, to identify the location of Walter Hicks's brewery, and formally - for instance on the livery of the transport fleet (see the photograph opposite). R.G. Barnes wrote to A.S.B. Payne in June 1934: *'Mrs Parnall and I are seriously considering the change of the name of the Company from Walter Hicks & Co. Ltd to St Austell Brewery Co. Ltd. This could conveniently be done at the present time when various other changes in the constitution of the Company are contemplated. Do you see any objection to the change? I am advising you of this beforehand so that you may*

keep down the stock of labels, crown corks, invoices, letter paper etc. to the minimum dimensions.'

The purchase of the venerable Ellis Brewery brought about a significant expansion of the business in the west of the county where all of its houses were located. The Ellis family had been brewing in Hayle since 1815, but the handsome buildings in use in the 1930s dated from 1873. Unusually extensive records of this once thriving company have survived; Paul Stephens, who has an exhaustive knowledge of Ellis history, describes how in its early days *'beer, wine and spirits would seem to have been almost less important than general trading and merchandising... At various times the brewery sold such diverse items as wheat, barley, apples, pigs, pipes, tobacco, reeds, clover, nails, white sugar, salt, malt and cheese.'* He also recounts the story of a rhyme which was supposedly to be found carved on a lintel in the Dolcoath Mine count house: *'If you don't drink Ellis' beer, You don't work here'!*

Therein, you could say, lay the source of this brewery's strength but also its ultimate downfall. The fortunes of the Ellis Brewery were shackled to those of the mines, the foundries and the shipyards of West Cornwall, an area whose economy had already been devastated and whose population decimated long before the final blow of the

ABOVE: *Christopher Ellis.* FAR RIGHT: *Tregrehan in 1928.*

Birth of a brand

In the late 1920s the Brewery's stock draught brews were XX, XXX, XXXX (bottled as Brown Willy Ale, named after Cornwall's highest hill), PA, BB (bottled as Light Ale) and IPA (India Pale Ale), but the Head Brewer Mr Smallwood was looking to develop a new stronger bottled beer to compete with the popular pale ales produced by Bass and Worthington. The following extracts from letters chart the progress of this new product whose name was to become a Brewery standard:

16th December 1927, Mr Gillett (Manager and Secretary 1927-30) to R.G.Barnes: *'I have been amusing myself trying to get out a new label for the higher gravity Beer we intend to put before the Trade. There is a great deal in the name and the difficulty is to get one "snappy" enough to "catch on". Mrs Parnall rather liked the name "Duchy". Should we be sailing too near the wind, as regards the triangle as I have shown it, which is, you know, Bass's trade mark? As an alternative to this, how would it be to substitute a map of Cornwall and on it mark in the Branches?'*

30th December, W.J. Cummins (printer) to the Brewery: *'I am enclosing herewith sketch of your Duchy Ale label. The colours are red and black to match your Crown Cork, but you could, if you desired, have the words "The Brewery, St Austell" in green.'*

4th January 1928, R.G. Barnes to Mr Gillett: *'I agree with Mrs Parnall in preferring the label marked with the red cross at the back, but I think this label could be considerably improved by a better drawing of the county of Cornwall. I have roughly traced on the covering paper the outline of Cornwall from an atlas which will shew you how much the draughtsman is out in getting the proper outline...'*

12th January, R.G. Barnes to Mr Gillett: *'The Controller of Trade Marks is not in favour of my proposal to register "Duchy" as our trade mark. Under the Act he is not allowed to register as a trade mark a word "according to its ordinary signification a geographical name". At any rate, if a formal application is turned down for us, it cannot be granted for anyone else, and I cannot think that if we start using the mark any decent brewer would imitate it. Thanks to Mr Smallwood we have got hold of a good name. The next thing is to produce a beer to match it, which is Mr Smallwood's job.'*

13th January, Mr Gillett to R.G. Barnes: *'I suggested to Mrs Parnall yesterday that it might be worth while to have a couple of gross or so of Show Cards, having in the centre an enlarged copy of our new label and printed on it, say, "Try our Duchy Ale. 6d per bottle" or something of that sort. I suggest that it should be hung in the Bars of Houses to draw customers' attention that there was something new about...I am putting in the first brew on Monday week, this should be ready for bottling about the time we shall probably receive the labels etc.'*

11th February, R.G. Barnes to Mr Gillett: *'Mrs Parnall and I have been discussing the Solasigns. We think for the Maxwells and the Durrant a smaller sign with DUCHY ALE only will be sufficient. For the larger waggons DRINK DUCHY ALE with DUCHY in silver.'*

14th February, Mr Gillett to R.G. Barnes: *'I have today sent to you per Passenger Train a case containing one dozen bottles of Duchy Ale. I think the beer will improve after being another ten days in cask; to me it seems at present somewhat green, but there is a nice hop palate. I asked them to enclose some Crown Cork openers in the case, as you may not have any.'*

6th March, Mr Smallwood to R.G. Barnes: *'You will be pleased to hear that I think Duchy Ale is going well, everyone is sending in repeat orders. We are racking another Brew tomorrow and on Friday are brewing again. A "gentleman" was seen to be making tracks for home (Mount Charles) a few evenings ago; he was not capable of demonstrating Euclid's definition of a straight line, and when he wobbled there were, I understand, cries of "Up Duchy!" "Up Duchy!"'*

It was a good name, and it still is; a new bottled Duchy was introduced (as Royal Duchy at first) in 1954 and ceased production in 1993, but the name lives on as by then it had been transferred to the award-winning keg bitter that was originally called Extra.

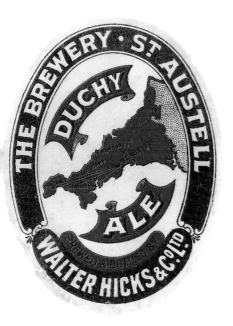

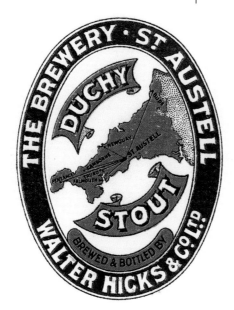

worldwide economic depression of the 1930s. Brewing ceased in 1934 and the Hayle brewery became St Austell Brewery's main depot in the west, as it remains today. Christopher Ellis junior, known as Chrissie, joined the board of St Austell Brewery as a salaried director, and preferential shares were issued to members of the Ellis family.

In the year 2000 Ellis beer was drunk again in Hayle for the first time in 66 years. St Austell's Head Brewer Roger Ryman brewed a special one-off ale from an Ellis recipe of 1872 discovered by Paul Stephens and took it to CAMRA's national festival in London; fittingly, it was also available at the Cornish Arms in Hayle, just across the road from the old brewery.

A year after the purchase of the Ellis Brewery, in which he had played such a key legal role, R.G.Barnes died aged 66; he had retired from Kent to Cornwall two years earlier and taken a lease on Trenarren House, but was given tragically little time to enjoy it. He was replaced on the Board by his son Egbert Barnes, the only surviving grandson of Walter Hicks.

In 1927 Hester had taken a lease on Tregrehan, the ancestral home of the Carlyon family, and here at last she found herself in a place that was grand enough to suit her. She lived at Tregrehan on and off (interspersed with sojourns in London and

Kent) until 1936 and was able to indulge her love of gardening in a long-established and historically important ornamental landscape. The garden at Tregrehan dates from the 1840s and later, and is considered by many to have the finest collection of exotic trees and shrubs in Cornwall.

Hester entertained some illustrious visitors here, most notably the Prince of Wales (later Edward VIII) and Mrs Simpson during one of their trips to Cornwall when they used to stay at the nearby Carlyon Bay Hotel (then called the St Austell Bay Hotel). Hester's great-nephew Tim Harvey recalls: *'I was terrified of Aunt Hester's butler at Tregrehan, and the fact that she had one! She was very keen on gardening, as was the Prince of Wales, and I think that's how she met him - she managed to inveigle him to come and see the gardens at Tregrehan and it became a great social feather in her cap.'*

Cecil Brewer, who worked at the Brewery from 1927 to 1975, remembers a grand fête held at Tregrehan in honour of the Prime Minister Stanley Baldwin. Hester, a lifelong Conservative supporter, had the Brewery shut down for the day so that everyone could (and had to!) attend the fête.

It was the first time that a Prime Minister had visited Cornwall during his tenure of office, and an estimated 20,000 people (and 800 motor vehicles) turned up at Tregrehan on that June day in 1927 to hear him speak. The *Cornish Guardian* described in detail the *'gigantic picnic'* held in the park, with stalls, roundabouts, trick-cycling, wrestling tournaments, athletic sports, tug-of-war competitions and clay target shooting. Three silver bands led the crowd in community singing (including 'Trelawny') and Hester Parnall judged the *'best decorated bicycle'* competition.

ABOVE RIGHT: *The Yacht, 1936, before rebuilding.* RIGHT: *The new Yacht in 1938.* ABOVE FAR RIGHT: *Aerial view of Penzance seafront, showing the Jubilee Pool and the Yacht.*

The Yacht Inn, Penzance

The Yacht was one of the 30 houses that came to the Brewery in 1934 with the purchase of the Ellis Brewery. Originally called the Mariner's Arms (*'and remembered as such by me'*, wrote Chrissie Ellis in 1929), it cost £1500 and was in a somewhat run-down state by that time, with only a beer-shop licence rather than a full one. In 1936 the Brewery appointed the Penzance architect Mr Drewitt, of Cowell, Drewitt and Wheatly, to rebuild the Yacht in a style to complement the nearby Jubilee Bathing Pool on the Promenade which had been opened in 1935. This fabulous open-air tidal lido, restored in 1990 and now a listed structure, was designed by Frank Latham, the Penzance Borough Engineer. It is memorably described by Roger Deakin in his wonderful book *Waterlog: 'With its dramatic ocean-liner decks, stainless-steel fittings, steps and tubular*

railings, the Jubilee Pool is highly theatrical...It is pure 1930s in its exuberant, extravagant use of concrete and in the flowing lines of its romantic, impractical shape.' The designs of the pool and the Yacht were strongly influenced by the Modernist movement in European architecture; they are both important historic structures and they bring to the Penzance seafront the unmistakeable *élan* of those pre-war years.

'"What a picture! A wonderful sight" ejaculated the Prime Minister as he stepped on the gaily-beflagged platform in the lovely grounds of Tregrehan and waved toward the green slope on which a great crowd cheered and waved flags and handkerchiefs in greeting. No more suitable spot for a great Cornish conservative demonstration could have been chosen than the residence of Mrs T. R. Parnall.' The *Cornish Guardian*.

In addition to her ever-present Pekingeses, Hester kept a Minah bird at Tregrehan which constantly used to repeat the words *'kiss me nice!'* Apparently it had learned the phrase from Hester's chauffeur who used to say it to the parlourmaids.

Hester Parnall died on 20th April 1939 at the age of 73. She had been troubled by painful ailments in her last years of life, including persistent rheumatism, and broke her hip in June 1938 (her immobility thereafter prevented her from living at Point Neptune in Fowey, which she had bought after leaving Tregrehan), but it seems that her fundamental health was good and her death took everyone by surprise. As late as 7th April she was still firmly in the saddle, writing briskly to Mr Payne to advise against buying German-made glass-lined tanks: *'I roused Mr Barnes this morning from his slumbers to give him my opinion about the tanks and he agrees with me that they should not be German.'*

Chrissie Ellis's letter of condolence to Egbert Barnes on hearing of her death serves as a heartfelt valediction to this remarkable woman: *'I don't know how to express my sorrow at the sad death of Mrs Parnall. I little thought when we met at St Austell a short time since that it was for the last time, she was so bright and cheerful then. It seems so hard after all she has gone through since last June and the brave way in which she faced it all that her good and useful life should terminate so abruptly. Please accept from my family and myself the deepest sympathy with you all in your sad loss.'*

RIGHT: *From left to right: Egbert Barnes, Kenneth Moore and George Luck.* ABOVE FAR RIGHT: *The stables on fire 12th June 1939.* FAR RIGHT: *The same view the following day.*

CHAPTER IV

Steady hands

Hester Parnall was succeeded as Chairman of the Brewery by Egbert Barnes; 1939 was to prove to be quite a year for this 41 year-old lawyer, who had had less than four years on the Board since his father died and now suddenly found himself in the hot seat. It was clear from the start, however, that Egbert was more than a match for the job; he was able to combine his father's thoroughgoing knowledge with a boundless enthusiasm for and loyalty to the Brewery and a delightfully irreverent and youthful sense of humour. In a letter of June 1938, A.S.B. Payne had cause to remind Egbert gently that he had not responded to Payne's earlier request to use the company seal on an excise entry. Egbert replied immediately, in the form of a telegram sent from Lords Cricket Ground: *'YES USE SEAL. AUSTRALIA 315 TO WIN'.* His forty years at the helm were to be ones of unforeseen challenge and change; that the Brewery not only survived but flourished during this time, and that everyone who remembers him does so with enormous respect and affection, are testimony to the character of this man.

Two months after Hester's unexpected death, the Brewery was to face another crisis when a serious fire broke out in the garages in the yard, supposedly caused by a Thornycroft lorry overheating. Cecil Brewer recalls that it was the eve of the Royal Cornwall Show and all the lorries were loaded up with beer ready to be taken to the show the following morning. It was a windy evening and before long the entire L-shaped range of buildings enclosing the yard to the south and east was aflame; here were housed the garages (formerly the stables), the carpentry and paint shops, the fitters' shop, and the highly inflammable paint store and timber store, along with the gatekeeper's cottage where Bill Burt and his family lived. The *Cornish Guardian* reported that: *'In the earlier stages of the fire, the bursting of the petrol tanks and the explosion of bottles had been*

reminiscent of the early stages of a bombardment in warfare and the flames were too fierce to approach to within 50 feet.' Despite this, a handful of Brewery employees managed to rescue furniture, as well as one lorry, a light van and two private cars. They were helped by cricketers who abandoned the game they had been playing nearby; Clifford Hockin recalled that *'amid cheers from the onlookers, first the cricketers and then the St Austell Boy Scouts arrived, formed a chain and helped remove the*

furniture from the cottage'. The town's new fire engine *Ruby* was on hand; it was her first outing but not a particularly auspicious one since the water pressure in the hydrants was so low that all that emerged from the hose was an ineffectual trickle which ran down the arm of fireman George Thomas. Eventually, water from the reservoirs up behind the Brewery was used to get the fire under control.

Many old Brewery records, which had been stored in boxes in the upstairs rooms, were lost in the fire along with the buildings themselves (later partially rebuilt at a cost of £795) and four new Bedford lorries. However the show had to go on, and four days later A.S.B. Payne was writing to Egbert Barnes in stalwart tones: *'In spite of all our troubles this week, trade is up 34 Barrels, which is quite satisfactory.'*

Less than five months after he had taken over as Chairman, Egbert had to face a very different crisis with the outbreak of war. Two days after Britain had declared war on Germany, Egbert wrote to A.S.B. Payne, whom he had promoted from Manager and Secretary to be the Brewery's first Managing Director: *'It's a great relief to my mind to know I have you in charge and in authority at the Brewery, and if any further justification of the appointment I was so glad to make as soon as I took over was needed - which it isn't - we certainly have it now. Keep me in touch as much as you can. It helps and cheers me to know how things are. Our maxim must be to go slow and cut out all frills till we see how things stand.'*

In July 1939 Egbert had made his priorities as Chairman of the Brewery quite clear in a written declaration of his thoughts and aims, which today might be described as his mission statement. Prophetically subtitled *'If Hitler lets us!'*, the list opens with: *'Our first and constant aim must be directed to raising wages to a*

RIGHT: *Egbert Barnes.*

Egbert's letters

28th September 1937, Egbert Barnes to A.S.B. Payne on receiving the routine monthly figures: *'August - "quite good"? August damn well magnificent! My heartiest congratulations to you and all concerned.'*

February 1943, Egbert Barnes to Claude Aylwin on the subject of interviewing prospective tenants for one of the Brewery's hotels: *'I was very favourably impressed by them. He is quite presentable; she must have been very nice looking; the daughter, a grass widow with a husband in the RAF, is very nice looking. (I imagine she was brought up with a view to impressing susceptible chairmen). They have no hotel experience at all... Mrs W. was emphatically confident that she could manage the catering and hotel side, and daughter, fixing her soulful eyes upon me and doing a bit of a flutter of the eyelids, said that her mother was a most competent person... Altogether I feel you will think that I am not a competent person to interview prospective hoteliers...'.*

Memories of Egbert

Clifford Hockin: *'A great leader, he was also an intensely human man with an infectious and almost schoolboy enthusiasm. "Crikey" and "Golly" were often among his exclamations of surprise or delight together with an acute yet splendidly broad sense of humour. He was always eager for advice and opinions yet when it came to the put-to he unhesitatingly accepted the responsibility for the ultimate decision. One of his senior staff once said of him "When things go right it is to us he gives the credit and when they go wrong he is the one who takes the blame"'.*

Cecil Brewer: *'Mr Barnes? He was a gentleman.'*

The Swastika stoppers

One bizarre effect of the rise of the Nazi party in Germany in the 1930s was that St Austell Brewery had to have all its old bottle tops (screw stoppers) drilled out or ground down to erase the image of a swastika with which they were stamped as a trade mark. When and why the Brewery adopted this symbol is not known, but the swastika had been used throughout history and by almost every culture in the world as a common decorative motif. Its meaning varied slightly from country to country and from faith to faith, but the origin of the word is from the Sanskrit for 'conducive to well being', and it was generally used as a token of good luck. However, ancient forms of the symbol tended to have it resting flat and with the arms facing anti-clockwise, whereas the swastika adopted by the German Nazi Party faced clockwise at a 45-degree angle. Curiously, the Brewery swastika also faced clockwise, as can be seen from the stoppers that survived.

decent minimum'. Further on, he suggests the idea of *'some sort of Brewery Council with the powers and duties laid down in the opening chapters of the Rowntrees book* The Human Factor in Business, *as far as it is applicable to a small business',* and muses that *'I shouldn't be surprised if everyone in the Brewery could not point out some small thing which, if altered, would improve his work or comfort. It may be no more than a window that rattles or a lack of light in some corner...'* This, then, was a very different creature from his predecessor; for Egbert Barnes the welfare of the workforce and the welfare of the company were inextricably linked, and his natural sense of justice and fair play meant that he wanted the best possible conditions for everyone.

He had nailed his colours to the mast early on, whilst his aunt was still Chairman, by encouraging her to introduce a company pension scheme in 1938, some time before most other comparable businesses had thought of such a thing. Based on a very small percentage of the weekly wage, plus the company's contribution, it produced an annual pension for each year of service plus free life assurance and disablement benefit during the year. Cecil Brewer remembers that the Brewery management took time and care to clarify this unfamiliar proposal: *'The pension scheme, it was Mr Barnes's idea and when they mooted it we used to go up in the bottling store and the whole brewery was there and somebody explained it to us. I think we had two or three meetings and you could pop questions if you wanted. Wages were very low, and they said you had to take so much a week out; but eventually we voted to have it - good thing too.'*

For the first six years of Egbert's Chairmanship, however, it was the war that dictated the course of Brewery business. The company had to learn how to operate with a restricted workforce and to adapt to shortages in raw materials and fuel and the loss, through requisition, of most of its transport fleet. Brewing was classified as an essential food industry; although excise duty was high, beer was not rationed and in fact breweries were encouraged to increase production in order to supply the troops and to maintain morale on the home front.

The sudden death of A.S.B. Payne in July 1942 was a particular blow; the calm expertise which he brought both to management and then to the Board had been enormously appreciated by Egbert in his difficult first years. Kenneth Moore, from the company's firm of auditors, had joined the Board in 1939 as a non-executive director, but now Egbert was left with an urgent need for a good reliable Managing Director at a time when manpower was in short supply. Soon after Payne's death he wrote this characteristically straightforward letter to Claude Aylwin, a man whom he had never met but who had been suggested to Kenneth Moore by a mutual acquaintance: *'You won't know me from Adam, nor will the signature at the foot of this leave you much wiser so I'll introduce myself as soon as possible. I am the Chairman of a small family brewery - the St Austell Brewery Co. - in Cornwall. Our Managing Director, one A.S.B. Payne, an awfully good chap, has died suddenly and we*

ABOVE: *Left to right: Jack Herbert, A. S. B. Payne and Kenneth Moore in 1935.*
ABOVE FAR RIGHT: *Wallpaper in the White Hart dining-room.* FAR RIGHT: *The Ship Inn, Pentewan, one of the houses previously owned by the Treluswell Brewery.*

The White Hart, St Austell

The White Hart had been St Austell's foremost inn for centuries, situated at first in Fore Street (where it was described by a traveller in 1799 as *'the best we had seen in Cornwall'*) before moving to its present grander premises in the early nineteenth century. Unlike so many houses that still bear the name, this is an inn in the proper sense of the word in that it provides accommodation. The splendid building started life as a town house for Charles

Rashleigh, who was responsible for the development of the port at Charlestown. At that time it was two-storied, but the Brewery added the top storey in 1925, having bought the White Hart in 1911 for £5000. Despite being the classiest establishment that St Austell had to offer, it still at that time had a notorious tap room which, the *St Austell Star* reported in 1912, *'was a habitual resort of prostitutes'.*

The famous French wallpaper dating from c.1800, which used to adorn the dining-room with Italian landscape scenes, was given by the Brewery to the British Museum in 1935. Hester Parnall wrote to A.S.B. Payne on the 1st December: *'I hope the B. Museum men have had some measure of success getting the paper off at the W. Hart. I am amazed at the interest it has caused. I daresay the Public think we have received a mighty sum for it, instead of being the other way round!'*

During the war the White Hart took on a new role that was to continue for many successful years, initiated by Egbert Barnes who had a particular interest in contemporary British art. In the summer of 1944 he organised, in conjunction with Borlase Smart and the St Ives Society of Artists, the first of many exhibitions of paintings at the White Hart. Over the years since then some of the best-known names in modern art have hung their works here, including Peter Lanyon, Augustus John, Paul Nash and Ben Nicholson. Extracts from the Foreword he wrote for that first show tell us much about Egbert's character and

guiding principles: *'This Exhibition of Pictures is an experiment, and this is why it is being made... I determined some ten years ago to make an effort to understand what the Artist of the present day was doing. I gave myself six months and if at the end of that time I could make nothing of him, I said I would give it up. I never have given it up. I was often mystified; I am often still mystified. But I have got a great deal of pleasure... Now how, even if he wants to, can a man follow the work of Contemporary Painters? It involves going round the small commercial galleries and seeing what is on, but they only exist in London. They are not much good to us in Cornwall. This, then, is an attempt to provide in St Austell something of the same facilities that exist in London, but with this difference: these pictures are priced by the Artists and we charge neither commission nor expenses for the Exhibition. If they are sold, purchasers can take them away on payment. For this reason the pictures will be continually changing (or so we hope)... We hope particularly that the Art Masters of any of our local schools will bring their students to see the pictures...'.*

In 1963 Egbert was amused to recall *'my colleagues' pained surprise'* when in 1946 he had bought two Ben Nicholson paintings for the Brewery for £50 and £30. Seventeen years later they were sold at Sotheby's for £2,350 and the proceeds paid for the entire refurbishment of the White Hart!

Recently the White Hart has had another important role to play in the life of the Brewery, and in the regeneration of St Austell, since its transformation into an award-winning training centre of excellence for the licensed trade and the wider hospitality business.

are looking for a successor...The object of this letter is to know if you would like to consider the job. I must tell you a little more about the company. Capital £250,000, the ordinary shares (£200,000) being all held by my family. No debentures. Barrelage about 25,000 a year. Profits round about the £40,000 mark. We've got a jolly good staff and a clever brewer in one Smallwood, though he's nearer 70 than 65, alas. I think I can say it's a thoroughly clean little business and I am sure that there are no skeletons in any of its cupboards. Payne used to run the show entirely and I had absolute confidence in him. I live in Wiltshire; we kept in touch mostly by telephone and I used to go down once a month or so to look around...'

Much to Egbert's relief, Aylwin took the job and, with the aid of the Company Secretary Mr Giles, ran the brewery efficiently through the remaining war years. In 1943 the Brewery entered into a rare alliance with its chief rival - the Redruth Brewery - to buy the Treluswell Brewery Company and its twelve tied houses. Brewing had ceased on Treluswell Hill, just outside Penryn, and the old brewery buildings were disposed of but St Austell was able to add six houses to its estate for a total of £15,000. Four more houses were bought during the war, three of which were important old coaching inns on main roads through the county: the Victoria at Roche, the London Inn at Summercourt and the Victoria at Threemilestone.

The Brewery by now had a large and scattered estate which, due to the restrictions of wartime, was in a poor state of repair.

As early as 1942 Egbert was thinking ahead, despite the uncertain outcome of the conflict. He ordered a survey of all the houses, working from Bude westwards, *'so that a programme of necessary repairs and desirable improvements and where necessary rebuilding might be drawn up ready to put into operation after the war.'* As the war drew to a close, the Board repeatedly voiced its concern about the visual and structural dilapidation of its houses and made it clear that this was to be the Brewery's post-war priority.

Plans were in place, but the Brewery's long-term programme of improvement and modernisation did not really get into gear until the advent of a new Managing Director who joined the company in 1946, succeeding Claude Aylwin on his retirement in the following year. The ensuing partnership between George Luck and Egbert Barnes was an extraordinary combination of longevity, commitment and friendship, and it gave the Brewery the strength and stability to survive the choppy waters of that unknown post-war world. In his memoirs, written for his children after retirement, George recalled how it all began: *'Egbert Barnes and I met for the first time in our long association at 9 o'clock on a Saturday morning in early August on Paddington Station. Before long he asked me what my plans were for the rest of the morning. "Nothing at all important" I replied, "but I had been hoping to go down to my parents in Sussex for the weekend which would mean I would be getting a train from Waterloo later on." "Capital!" exclaimed Egbert. "I want to go to Waterloo too; let's walk there shall we?" And so we did, talking non-stop the whole way. It is fair to say that we got on well together from the first moment and fortunately continued to do so for the next 33 years until we both retired in 1979.'* George found out later that he had been something of a late entrant; there had been 200 applicants for the job (advertised as *'General Manager,*

RIGHT: *George Luck with his wife Diana and three eldest sons, 1955.*
FAR RIGHT: *The Fox and Hounds, Comford.* ABOVE FAR RIGHT: *Brewery lorry* c. *1948.*

Memories of George Luck

Cecil Brewer: 'He used to go around the Brewery every Friday afternoon and have a chat with everyone, see everyone, called everyone by their Christian names. He was different; you could talk to him.'

Clifford Hockin: 'He would call regular meetings of the whole Brewery to hear everyone's views, and so that everyone knew what was happening. When he walked round on Friday afternoons he knew everyone and had a word for them all; he thought about people and remembered everything about them.'

Tim Harvey: 'George had the foresight to see how the future was going to go, and he had the biggest influence on the Brewery expanding on the wines and hotels side. He'd been a traditional brewer before the war, but he saw that the company needed to embrace all sorts of other skills and ideas rather than just brewing gallons and gallons of beer. He was a great traditionalist in lots of ways, but he was also very forward looking.'

Doing a proper job

6th June 1938, letter from Hester Parnall to A.S.B. Payne: *'I heard from Mr Barnes this morning, he caught a glimpse of the sign of the Welcome Home as he passed over the Railway Bridge, and agrees with me that the white frame is hopeless, it must be black - I forgot to see if there was any old decorative iron at the Brewery which could be used to make the post look less like a gibbet...'*

From an article, 'Signs of the Good Inn', in *Country Town* 1947: *'Mr Luck, general manager of the St Austell Brewery Co., says that the company's view is that inn signs should be an integral part of the countryside... "If that is so", he says, "it is worth taking trouble with the signs, designing and painting them well, and having the ironwork of the brackets made, as ours are, by a real craftsman".'*

From *St Austell: Church, Town, Parish* by Dr A.L. Rowse, 1960: *'We owe a great debt to the St Austell Brewery for its visual appeal... for wherever one is in Cornwall, one can recognise its inns by the excellence of their treatment, good taste in colour-wash and paint, a really beautiful lettering in black and gold, admirably painted inn-signs by good artists under their patronage. We can recognise and be proud; for a generation now St Austell Brewery has set this good example, been a patron of the arts - to its managers we owe the pictures in the White Hart and occasional exhibitions of paintings.'*

with prospects of promotion to Managing Director'), and Egbert had actually been on his way to Waterloo to offer the job to someone else, so that was a crucial walk they took on that Saturday morning.

George had trained as a brewer before the war, and since leaving the army had been working as an Outside Manager for Taylor Walker & Co. at their Barley Mow Brewery in Limehouse (a splendid building which, like St Austell, was designed by Inskipp and Mackenzie; it was demolished in the 1960s). At 32 some thought him too young and inexperienced for management, his career having been rudely interrupted by six years distinguished service overseas, but they were won round by Egbert's instinct that he was the right man for the job. On George's first visit to the Brewery, Egbert was keen that he should have a chance to look around before making a final decision: *'We were met at St Austell station by Howard Henwood, the first St Austell Brewery man I ever met, and the first Brewery pub I saw was the Cornish Arms (or Fifteen Balls as it was known) from the window of the train at Par. It looked rather drab but I was at once impressed by the distinction and simplicity of the gold and black lettering of the sign. The first pub I visited was the Crown Inn at St Ewe. Our tenant there was a hard-bitten,* *tough and forthright Cornishman and I remember his words when I was introduced as the prospective new manager. "Well b****r!" he said to Egbert. "He's a cheerful looking b****r anyway, which is more than what the other b****r is, b****r 'ee".'*

George's mention of the characteristic gold and black lettering touches upon a significant aspect of the Brewery's history. When he and Egbert began the mammoth task of redecorating and upgrading all the public houses, the one thing they did not have to do was to create or invent a visual identity for the company. They simply had to return to and reinforce something that had been in place from the early days: a concern for style and good quality that was intrinsic to the work of the Brewery's carpenters, masons, painters and signwriters.

The improvement programme was underway by 1946. In October of that year Egbert scribbled in a P.S. to a letter to Aylwin: *'Gold Leaf supplies - Have we a lot in stock? I foresee a complete re-writing of nearly all our signs.'* In the following month the Board confirmed the appointment of Mrs Betty Nagelschmidt *'to undertake responsibility for exterior decoration of the Company's properties'* and *'the*

adoption for all purposes of Trajan Column lettering', whilst noting *'that exterior decorations had been carried out at a total of approximately 60 houses in the last 18 months'.*

The appointment of Mrs Nagelschmidt was a bit of a *coup* for the Brewery (more specifically for Egbert Barnes, through his contacts in the art

ABOVE: *The Welcome Home at Par, one of Joy Cooper's most popular signs.*
ABOVE FAR RIGHT: *The Lifeboat Inn, St Ives: a new design by the current Brewery signwriter Andrew Grundon.*

The Smugglers story

One of the Brewery's most popular, and notorious, brews over the years started life as E.S.A. (Extra Strong Ale). With a barley wine flavour and an original gravity of 1060° (upped to 1070° in 1960), it was brewed for the Christmas trade in 1948 and was at first available only as a draught ale, sold at 2/4 a pint. In the following year, draught sales were discontinued and it was sold instead as Smugglers Ale in 'nip' bottles at 1/- each. As Clifford Hockin commented: *'Coming as it did, after the war with its lower gravity beers, a strong ale was eagerly anticipated and received with much acclaim.'* Soon afterwards, Egbert gleefully reported to the shareholders that: *'All beer, we know, is good: can we be right in thinking that some may be a little better than others? Smugglers, "Strong Ale of Cornwall", achieved a real success, and did our resources permit, it would be tempting to see if we could not sell it beyond the Tamar against all comers. Be that as it may we had it ready in time; it was a novelty to our visitors last year for few other Breweries were then brewing a strong ale'.* In 1952 Smugglers went to London, having been chosen to stock the model village pub in the Ideal Home Exhibition at Olympia.

The Smugglers story only came to an end in 1994, due to the planned closure of the bottling line. Smugglers had a fanatically loyal following, particularly down west, so how did they take the bad news? *'They've never forgiven us...'* said a Brewery insider darkly.

Smugglers Lament by D.W.E. of Fowey
From Praze-an-Beeble to Polperro, Sennen to Saltash,
There's Cornish drinkers in despair, and many teeth do gnash.
All those who liked a nifty nip
Will surely get the blues,
When they hear the awful tidings and digest the ghastly news.

The Brewery has killed it off, and Smugglers is no more,
It's followed all the Princes who left the Cornish shore.
We liked that little bottle,
Its contents tasted right,
And half a dozen, drunk at speed, could almost make you tight!

I'll bet t'was an accountant that did the dirty deed -
Not a proper drinking man, and probably a weed!
So farewell King of Prussia,
The Lugger and the New,
For Bosun's is no substitute for what we loved and knew.

I'd like to find out who it was, and meet him on the quay.
I doubt that I'd resist the urge
To shove him in the sea!

The sign of the Four Lords, St Blazey Gate

Joy Cooper painted this intriguing sign during the war. Due to various mishaps, the Brewery had had to wait for it for nearly three years. In October 1941 Joy wrote to Egbert: *'I hope your nerves are in a strong enough condition to withstand the shock of hearing that the "Four Lords" is, once more, finished and on its way to St Austell?!! My one terror is that anything should happen to it again - as easily it might, with the railways in their present condition - but it would be more than I could bear! It was extraordinarily difficult to find anywhere to paint it - once we'd left Wellington - and my hopes of doing it there were dashed, as it only arrived from the makers two days before we were going, and I had to dash to the station and square it up and draw out the design (for the guilders) on the spot...After that the guilders graciously kept it for nearly a year as, when I finally landed up here, the place was choc-a-block with evacuees! However, eventually someone died, and I managed to secure a few square feet in the middle of a lot of junk in what had once been a studio - hence the masterpiece was painted - at last! There is one important thing - it must be hung (not kept indoors) for three months and then varnished - this is vital. Also the varnish must not cover the gold, so it will have to be done very carefully... I should imagine all the others will need re-varnishing by now - they ought to be done annually without fail.'*

The design itself has excited much interest and debate over the years. The 'Four Lords' are the four main landowners in the area, whose manorial boundaries met at St Blazey Gate. As to their actual identities - well you can take your pick from the landed families of Carlyon, Edgcumbe, Rashleigh, Treffry, Roberts, Pearce, Polkinghorne, Rogers and Agar-Robartes, depending on the date when the pub's name was established. The story goes that the four lords of the manors of Biscovey, Trenovissick, Roselyon and Tregrehan used to meet regularly on 'neutral ground' at this inn which was a notorious gambling den, and that on one occasion one of them lost so heavily that he had to sell a valuable ring to pay his gambling debts (hence Joy's double-sided sign which features the ring on one side but not on the other).

world). Better known by her maiden name of Elisabeth Benjamin, before the war she had been an architect of some distinction, a contemporary of Lubetkin and the Tecton group, much influenced by Le Corbusier and Gropius, and one of the few notable female exponents of the Modern Movement in Britain. No doubt it was she who encouraged the

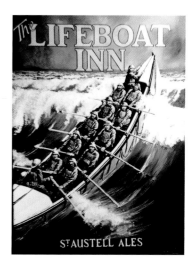

Brewery to employ Hans Feibusch, who was well known within London architectural circles, to decorate the Ship in Fowey with exterior murals (see p. 21). In an interview given in 1995 (Lynne Walker, in *Twentieth Century Architecture 2*) she recalled: *'After the war, when we were in Cornwall [1945-49], I was very friendly with Ben [Nicholson] and Barbara [Hepworth] and through them I got a job with the St Austell Brewery Company. They weren't allowed to build anything then because the restrictions were so severe, but I got out plans for development and I oversaw decoration and commissioned pub signs which was great fun.'*

Several different artists were employed over the years to design and paint the pictorial pub signs that are such a distinctive feature of the Brewery's houses, including Meriel Cardew (wife of the potter Michael Cardew), Crosby Cook and, most notably and prodigiously, Joy Cooper. Particularly after the war, encouraged by Egbert and George, these modern artists were being commissioned not just to churn out a traditional Queen's Head but to use their imagination. Between them, they are responsible for some of Cornwall's most striking and familiar examples of public art.

In 1951 the Brewery celebrated its Centenary. A special Walter Hicks Centenary Ale was brewed by Mr Minchin, who had been Head Brewer since Smallwood's retirement during the war; Centenary Port and Sherry were also produced. The highlight of the celebrations for Brewery staff was a weekend trip to London to visit the Festival of Britain Exhibition, travelling in four 'char-a-bancs' and taking over an entire hotel in Kensington on the Saturday night.

Another celebratory gathering was the dinner and dance for all the Brewery's tenants and managers which was held at the Hotel Bristol in Newquay. More than 250 people attended and, among the speeches, the health of the Brewery was proposed by Leslie Hawken, the landlord of the Cornish Arms at St Merryn. He presented Egbert Barnes with a clock from the managers and tenants of the company *'as a token of the high regard and esteem and deep affection in which they held the board of the company'.*

It was in this period that the wines and spirits side of the Brewery was practically reinvented. Although old Walter had been a wine and spirit merchant before he was a brewer, it had since become merely a junior element of the company with a very limited stock - mostly spirits - sold only to the Brewery houses. Although it would have been hard to foresee the extraordinary rise in popularity of wine drinking in this country in the next half century, Egbert and George had the good sense to recognise that this was an undeveloped aspect of the business that had some potential.

Tim Harvey, Walter Hicks's great-grandson, was responsible for expanding and enhancing the stock out of all recognition, and for relaunching it under a rather familiar trading name. At the Board Meeting in October 1954 *'it was decided to operate the*

RIGHT: *A county map drawn for the Brewery to mark its Centenary, 1951.*
FAR RIGHT: *Egbert Barnes at a wine-tasting in the cellars, 1960.*

Brewery outings

The Centenary trip to London was one in a long line of annual Brewery outings, a tradition that went back to the early days. In 1925 the entire Brewery decamped to London on the train to visit the British Empire Exhibition. Clifford Hockin described how *'one of the highlights still remembered was of 'Happy' Dickie Davies ordering a pint of "Hicks" in a London pub'* (and being most put out that they hadn't heard of it...). Cecil Brewer remembered twice going to London with the Brewery in the 1930s; *'...and someone got tickets together to go the Morris Cowley works in Oxford - they put on some do for us. Then we went up to London in the evening, on the train, and went to see a show in the West End.'*

That sounds pretty civilised, but in general the outings, particularly in the '20s and early '30s, had a reputation for being riotous affairs. The usual pattern was to go by char-a-banc or train to Penzance or Plymouth, with the Brewery paying everyone's fare, plus 5/- spending money (*'quite a fair bit of money in they days'* remembers Cecil) and cigarettes or tobacco for the smokers. A letter to Hester Parnall from Mr Gillett in August 1929 hints at quite a story: *'Your staff met this morning and came to the decision to ask the Directors to allow them to fix the date of their Annual*

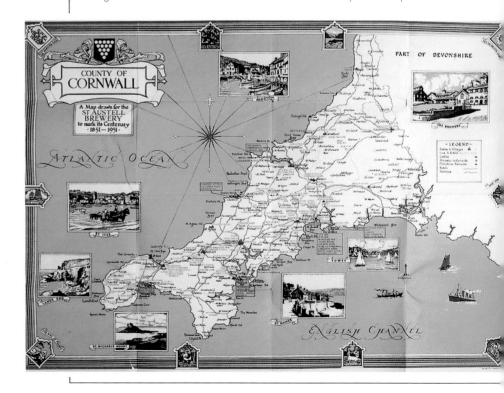

Outing for Saturday the 17th instant, this being the first day of Plymouth Naval Week. They also ask me to suggest that they be allowed to use a Char-a-banc for the journey, and would like to point out that the staff now contains no one who will be likely to abuse this privilege and cause unnecessary stops to obtain drink. It will also enable them to have the chance of having a pleasant drive, as they would like to go to Plymouth via a portion of Dartmoor.'

Egbert's centenary speech

In his extended Chairman's Statement to the AGM in that Centenary Year, a shortened version of which he gave as his address at the Newquay dinner, Egbert dwelt at length on the achievements of his grandfather and the challenges the Brewery faced a century on. *'The Duke of Wellington, that very practical old man, still alive in 1851, used to say that "All the business of war, and indeed all the business of life, is to endeavour to find out what you don't know by what you do; that's what I call guessing what is at the other side of the hill." That is certainly our business. Compared to the very mountains in front of us how easy looks the slope which confronted Walter Hicks! No income tax, no profits tax, no death duties, no interferences by busybodies, governmental or other, no permits, no rationing; an age, in fact, of self-help with profits counted as its due reward. Furthermore an age of expansion, of confidence, of rising population and rising standards of living. Looking back how easy it seems! But we must remember that Walter Hicks could not see the other side of his hill, however slight a slope it now looks from here. He had few reserves and no experience; his only positive assets were enterprise, adaptability, and the courage to take risks... Conditions are different now, but the qualities we should bring to bear on them must be the same. I think I can claim them on behalf of all who are working at the Brewery... They are a fine lot, a happy family and a good team. Let us be grateful to them one and all.'*

Wine and Spirit Department in future in the name of Walter Hicks & Co., primarily for the purposes of retail and private wine and spirit trade. At the same time we would increase the range of wines and spirits which we bottled ourselves, and bottle a number of them under our own labels.' From the mid-'50s onwards, regular wine-tastings for free trade customers were held in the atmospheric candle-lit shadows of the cellars.

Tim remembers that *'we were trying to set up a new identity, to attract the free trade and hotels and so on, and so when we produced our first promotional material - price lists and things like that - we used elements of the family coat of arms on it.'* This was the first appearance of the 'castle', taken from the Hicks arms on the memorial tablet in Luxulyan Church, which later came to represent the Brewery as a whole and is now such a strong and recognisable symbol of the company.

Today Walter Hicks & Co. is one of the Brewery's great success stories and offers the most comprehensive selection of wines and spirits available anywhere in the West Country. As well as stocking all the big names, the company also sells its own brands: Pendennis, Tintagel and Castle D'Or sherries, Walter Hicks Gin, Montpelier Plantation White Rum, Walter Hicks Navy Rum, Sabre Vodka, Mena Dhu Whisky and Western Hunt Ruby Port.

One of the reasons why Walter Hicks Wine Merchants is able, both financially and logistically, to hold such a large range of stock is because it has its own purpose-built bonded warehouse (the only one in Cornwall) which enables huge quantities of wines to be stored with duty unpaid until the last possible minute. In 1973 the storage capacity for wines and spirits was greatly increased during major building works at the Brewery, which sadly spelt the end of the delightful garden which had been Egbert's pride and joy. A new bond was connected to the original cellars by a tunnel excavated beneath the Brewery yard. By the turn of the century, it had again been outgrown and a brand new stand-alone bonded warehouse was built behind the Brewery in June 1999. The current

ABOVE: *Aerial view of the Brewery, late 1940s/early 1950s, showing the garden bottom right.*

The '125' story

In recent years the most famous product of Walter Hicks Wine Merchants has been the Walter Hicks '125' Navy Rum which, at 125° proof (71.4% vol.), is the strongest commercially-bottled rum available anywhere in the UK. Arriving directly from Guyana in 45-gallon barrels known as hogsheads, the rum is left to mature for seven years in the Stygian gloom of the Brewery's original bonded warehouse cellars, alongside wooden cases of vintage clarets and ports. At the end of this time, some of the matured rum is broken down with water to produce the 40% vol. brand, but for the '125' it is simply bottled as it is, at full strength, with nothing added and nothing taken away. It's a wonder that the bottles don't crack...

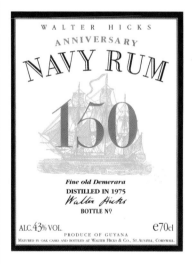

To celebrate the Brewery's 150th anniversary the range has been extended by a limited run of a 25-year-old rum at a strength of 43% vol. Only 1,212 bottles have been produced from this 1975 distillation which has been maturing in hogsheads ever since, developing into a spirit of rare finesse and distinction - a must for every rum buff.

Snippets from the board

1953/4 '...we must unfortunately reckon on meeting the competition of TV during the coming twelve months. I am told that the craze for viewing is all absorbing for the first six months and then, as it begins to wear off, old habits and pleasure gradually reassert themselves again. If so that threat is not so serious. But the cost of the set is another matter. Hire-purchase terms involve payments of about £1 a week for 18 months, a formidable competitor for the spare cash of most working families.'

1954/5 'We have secured the sole agency for Cornwall of 'Coca-Cola' so that if these Cola drinks become popular we will be selling the best, and the best known, of them.'

The Bishop & Wolf, St Mary's

Although the emphasis during this time was on consolidation and renovation rather than on buying new houses, the Brewery did make some strategic purchases in parts of the county where they had hitherto had little representation. One of these areas was the Isles of Scilly, where there was also a need for a depot to supply the free trade customers on the islands. In 1958 Egbert, George and Tim Harvey went to St Mary's to view a shop and house for sale in Hugh Town, with the idea of converting them to a public house. They reported back that *'the shop was rather on the small side but was well placed and readily convertible. There was a fair sized garden at the rear with access on to a back road, making readily feasible the provision of a wholesale store.'*

Purchase and conversion eventually cost the Brewery around £18,000, and the Bishop and Wolf opened for Whitsun 1959, bearing the name of the famous lighthouses that lie to the south-west and east, respectively, of the Scillies. The two-sided pictorial pub sign is one of Joy Cooper's most striking designs. Today, the depot behind the pub is still a vital link to the Brewery's most remote customers, and regular replenishment comes by ship from Penzance Harbour.

stock list includes an exclusive list of 40 vintages of Growth clarets, 38 vintage ports, and wines from more than 20 countries - everywhere from Uruguay to Totnes!

The experimental introduction of Extra, the Brewery's first keg beer, in 1953 was *'a big innovation'*, according to Tim Harvey. *'In fact we were one of the first breweries in the country to do it. Watney's Red Barrel was the leader in that field and Watney's had a large amount of trade in Cornwall and so we thought - let's do it too! It did not really involve new technology as such - essentially it was just bottled beer in much bigger bottles - but we needed new ways of dispensing it and of course new tanks for chilling and filtering (these two processes being unheard of for draught beer).'*

By this time bottled beers were booming, as draught ales had an unreliable reputation; quality varied from brew to brew and they were sensitive to the differing skills of individual publicans. As Peter Voelcker, another of Walter Hicks's great-grandsons who joined the Brewery in 1959, put it: *'Unless you knew the landlord well you wouldn't risk the draught beer. Keg of course was much safer.'* Thus Extra was almost bound to be a success story, but Egbert and George were cautious at first because they were somewhat ahead of the field and the financial outlay was considerable. At a Board Meeting late in 1954, *'A report was given of the progress of the experimental stages in the production and sales of this beer. After discussion the Board decided to proceed with full-scale production, accepting the risk that the beer might be sold at the expense of our bottled beers or existing draught beers, and the outlay which would be required on plant and equipment.'* The total outlay was estimated at £20,000 - quite a steep amount for this prudent management team - but within two years it was clear that, as they had hoped, Extra was a huge hit with the free trade. As Egbert reported in 1956: *'The marketing of a stronger beer, known as Extra, and its*

distribution in stainless steel containers has been an unqualified
success and has brought us many new accounts and customers.
These containers are expensive, but they are a most convenient
and hygienic way of distributing beer and of serving it in the
best possible conditions.'

Extra went down well on the national stage too. In 1960 it was
on sale in London at Moore's Restaurant in Throgmorton Street,
and in 1976 it won a prestigious gold medal at a national beer
competition run by the *Sunday Mirror*, up against 312 beers
from 88 other breweries. Then in 1985 its name was changed
(*'people thought it sounded like a brand of petrol'*) to that old
Brewery standard 'Duchy', which had been used for the bottled
version of Extra since 1954.

In the early 1960s the company was shaken by the untimely
deaths of two key members of staff. Ian Turnbull had been

Company Secretary since 1952
and joined the Board in 1961.
His sudden death at the age of
56 came only a few months after
that of 42-year-old David Payne
(the son of A.S.B. Payne), who
had been assistant to Mr Minchin
before taking over as Head
Brewer in 1957. Egbert's son-in-
law David Staughton was
brought in on the Board, whilst
Alan Izat and Clifford Hockin
ably took over the roles of Head
Brewer and Company Secretary, but the loss of these two men
was keenly felt as Egbert made clear in this moving tribute to
David Payne: *'In the first place he was a thoroughly competent*

ABOVE: *Board member Scott Seaward, left, with David Payne.* CENTRE RIGHT: *Willie Warren
behind the bar of the Radjel.* ABOVE FAR RIGHT: *David Staughton.* BELOW FAR RIGHT: *Peter
Voelcker, above, and Piers Thompson.*

The gift of the Gribbin

In 1965 the National Trust launched Enterprise Neptune, its appeal to save the coastline. In
June of that year, Egbert Barnes wrote as a P.S. to his annual Chairman's Statement: *'May I
commend to Shareholders' generosity the National Trust's Enterprise Neptune to save as much as
possible of what is left of the Country's coastline? Nowhere is that more important than it is in
Cornwall'.* Characteristically he backed up his words with action, as Michael Trinick, who ran
the Trust in Cornwall, recorded in 1966: *'Mr E.C. Barnes, who is chairman of the St Austell
Brewery Company which already supports our Cornwall Coast Fund with a handsome Deed of
Covenant, asked if he and the company could help to buy the Gribbin, of which he is particularly
fond and which can be seen in the distance from his board room.'*

The gift was completed the following year, and Egbert and the Brewery thus helped to
secure one of Cornwall's loveliest headlands, one protective arm of St Austell Bay, for ever
and for everyone to enjoy.

The Radjel Inn, Pendeen

On March 29th 1973 a pub called the Boscaswell Inn, which had been owned by the Brewery since 1934, was renamed The Radjel in honour of its much-loved landlord Willie Warren on his 72nd birthday. A 'radjel' means a pile of stones where a fox makes its home, and it had been the nickname of Willie's great-great-grandfather.

A large photograph of Willie Warren's beaming face hangs on the wall of the Managing Director's office in the Brewery, amongst the soberly clad directors of the past. Willie died in 1980 at the age of 79 and still holds the Brewery record for the longest-serving landlord, having run The Radjel for 59 years. It was something of a family tradition. Willie had taken on the licence after the death of his grandmother who had been the licensee since her husband died; all told, Willie's family ran the pub for 99 years. His grandfather, William Maddern, had come to the Boscaswell Inn as landlord in 1881, and Willie was brought up there after his father – who was landlord of the Star Inn, St Just – died when he was two. By the time he was fourteen Willie was working down Levant Mine, but he left to help his grandmother at the pub following the man-engine disaster of 1919 when 31 miners lost their lives.

Brewer and to him is due, in a very large measure, the success of Extra. The men in the Brewery respected, trusted and - it is hardly too much to say - loved him. In the Board Room we did no less, besides having a high regard for his opinion and his judgement. Off duty his charm of manner, sense of humour and sporting activities made friends wherever he went - for the Brewery as its Ambassador as well as for himself.'

Other important changes of staff at this time were the arrival in the Brewery of two more of Walter Hicks's great-grandsons: Peter Voelcker and Piers Thompson. Tim Harvey had left to pursue a career in the wine trade in London and, his workload having expanded to beyond the capabilities of one man, Peter took over management of Walter Hicks & Co. whilst Piers was responsible for the Brewery's estate and free trade sales.

The Brewery built its one and, so far, only purpose-built pub in 1969 just off Tregonissey Road on what was then still the eastern outskirts of St Austell. The town was beginning to grow rapidly to the east and it was recognised that a pub would be needed to serve this massive area of new housing, as well as the newly-built head office of English China Clays close by. The entire project cost £36,343 and the William Cookworthy, named in honour of the Devonian chemist who had discovered Cornwall's reserves of china clay, was opened on

May 2nd. In the course of trying to decide upon a name, George Luck had written to local dignitaries asking for their opinions; one of them was that famous son of St Austell Dr A.L. Rowse whose characteristic retort was: *'William Cookworthy? No - I think you should call it the Rowse Arms!'*

In the mid-1970s the Brewery reached its peak barrelage since the war, thanks largely to exceptionally good summer weather and to the tourist boom (Cornwall's visitor numbers also peaked in the 1970s). Since that high point, the nation's traditional drink has been on the decline, nudged out by the popularity of wine and foreign lagers and the changes in social drinking brought about by the decline of heavy industry and manual labour. This was not the only fundamental change in the air as the time drew near for Egbert and George to retire. They had steered the Brewery safely through a period of major reorganisation in the brewing industry, when many small independent breweries were swallowed up by the nationals, but there was an even greater restructuring still to come. Thatcherism was on the horizon, and the mood of the country and within the business world was changing; although they had faced many challenges and difficulties in those post-war years, looking back from where we are today theirs seems by contrast to have been a gentle and a gentlemanly world.

The business principles of Egbert and George

At the AGM in 1953, Egbert gave what was in effect a statement of fundamental Brewery policy that held good for his and George Luck's entire period at the helm. In outlining how best to counter the increasing threat and competition from the national brewers, he said: *'As we see it our answer is to pursue with energy and determination the policy we have been adopting over the last few years. Our houses must be good to look at, comfortable and up to date in their amenities; our beers must be sound and well presented; we must neglect no chance of developing our valuable wine and spirit business; the sale of minerals must be expanded till it covers the county; our hotel business must not stand still for a moment. All these have been our objectives of recent years. Without them it may be safely said that our level of profits would have followed the general curve of sales in the industry. With them firmly in mind and steadily pursued we believe we can look after any competition.'*

And in 1961, these stirring words which are a fitting tribute to the era of Egbert and George: *'There are certain matters for which we owe thanks to all our staff: good management, good products, good service and, most valuable of all, the good will earned thereby. In these essential qualities we believe the small firm has advantages the huge can envy. To be best one need not be big - as long as one remembers that the best can always be bettered. By present day standards we are a small Brewery but we are proud of the beers we brew and of the wines we sell, of our Houses, of the men and women who work for us and of the reputation we believe these things have brought us. We hope that you are too.'*

RIGHT: *The Brewery staff float in St Austell Carnival, 1949.*
FAR RIGHT: *The Brewery, 1979.*

CHAPTER V

Growing and brewing

In 1979 Egbert was succeeded as Chairman by his son-in-law David Staughton, and Piers Thompson took over from George Luck as Managing Director. George's son Adam Luck, meanwhile, had joined the Brewery in 1975 with responsibility for the tenanted trade, and in 1980 James Staughton (Walter Hicks's great-great-grandson) came in on the wines and spirits side. In this new age, which was altogether more demanding and competitive, it was time for the Brewery's priorities to shift and develop. Egbert and George had created a solid foundation; the estate of pubs and hotels was in good order and the company finances were sound, thanks to their intrinsic prudence. Now Piers and his fellow directors (initially just his cousin Peter Voelcker, but joined by Michael Ruthven in 1987 who came with a wide brewing and retail experience) could see that the business needed to grow in order to survive and go forward.

The first area of growth was in the Brewery's estate, which had expanded very little since the war. This meant not simply buying more pubs, but having a strategic policy. Piers had already made some key acquisitions such as the Pandora Inn at Restronguet, the Great Western Hotel at

Newquay and the Old Customs House at Padstow which were proving to be very successful; now the Brewery looked to expand into Devon. In the last twenty years depots serving the free trade have been opened up in Ilfracombe, through buying the Drink Link company, and in Newton Abbot, and fifteen Devonian houses have been bought - the furthest east being the Mill on the Exe at Exeter. At the start of 2001 the Brewery bought its 152nd pub - the Victoria Inn in Salcombe - for £1 million; whatever would Walter Hicks have made of that? Hand in hand with acquisition has been a programme of investment in the larger managed houses to allow them to reach their full potential and to keep pace with the increased expectations of their customers. Pubs like the Central in Newquay, the Old Customs House in Padstow and, more recently, the Pedn-Olva Hotel in St Ives have had considerable sums spent on their redevelopment, with immediate returns justifying the expenditure.

LEFT: *The Harbour Inn, Porthleven.* ABOVE: *The Pedn-Olva Hotel, St Ives.*
ABOVE RIGHT: *The Mill on the Exe, Exeter.*

Growth in business was the next priority to be addressed, and in 1993 the Brewery took one of the most significant steps in its history when it bought Carlsberg-Tetley's wholesale business in Cornwall and the Isles of Scilly. In an era increasingly dominated by choice and diversity, this major investment has allowed the Brewery to compete profitably in the free trade as composite wholesalers, with the ability to supply its customers with all their liquid requirements in one delivery. *'It was the biggest single change in our direction'* recalls Adam Luck of the Carlsberg-Tetley deal, for which the Brewery could thank Piers Thompson's *'vision, sound business sense and extraordinarily good judgement'*. James Staughton was responsible for masterminding the complex deal itself. *'It meant that we could go to free houses and clubs and so on not only with our own brands to offer them, but the national brands which are Carlsberg-Tetley products, and then say: this is what we've got to offer. It's given us a wide portfolio, and it has been incredibly successful.'*

ABOVE: *The Brewery laboratory.* ABOVE RIGHT: *The copper (1914-1998).*
FAR RIGHT: *Roger Ryman.*

The pull of a good pint

Letter to the *Cornish Guardian* from Mr Cyril Thompson of Fowey, August 1981: *'A disaster has struck the people of Cornwall. Our adorable St Austell Brewery have increased the price of their excellent beer by 3p per pint. Thousands, including myself, will have no option than to join a club or form social clubs where we can get our couple of pints 4p to 5p cheaper. We all know the quality of the beer that this family brewery have brewed for years, but they must understand that people cannot afford to pay the price tag on their products. So farewell to all St Austell brewery houses, until the day you decide to reduce your beer to a reasonable price. We shall all be wearing black ties, and going into mourning for one month, out of respect for the excellent services, beautiful beer and comfort of the St Austell brewery pubs, which we have enjoyed for so many years and which we are now deprived of by the abominable, diabolical, outrageous 3p per pint increase. One man's loss is another man's gain in the brewery trade.'*

Letter to the *Cornish Guardian* from Mr Cyril Thompson of Fowey, September 1981: *'Recently I wrote a letter compaining about the 3p increase in the price of a pint of St Austell brewery's beer. I stated that I would never again drink this beer. But I am a man of honour and never afraid to stand corrected. I feel I have made a mistake. The price of beer in the club bars may be a few pence cheaper. But after visiting a number of clubs I have gone back to my beloved pint of wonderful and delicious St Austell brew...and back to my local public house. I was only away for a week - but how I missed my excellent landlord and landlady. Now I am happily and contentedly back in the fold.'*

Farewell to old friends?

In 1998 the old 100-barrel copper, which had been boiling away steadily since 1914, was replaced by a stainless steel giant with a 150-barrel capacity. Unlike the two original steam-heated 40-barrel coppers (one of which is still in use today) this one was coal-fired, presumably because at the time of the 1912-14 expansion the Brewery's boilers were not large enough to cope with the increased workload. In this great open cauldron, built into a kiln made from 10,000 local bricks (it received a copper lid in 1947 and was later converted to steam), the wort and hops were boiled over a constantly-tended coal fire for an hour and a half. In between brews the copper was scrubbed out by hand using two buckets of fine sand; for this gruelling work the boilermen were given double the daily allowance of pale ale (two quarts). At the end of its working life, the copper lives on through recycling: it has been used to make commemorative copper coins to celeberate the Brewery's 150th anniversary.

As various elements of the Brewery have been replaced or renewed over the years, so some have inspired more nostalgia than others. Few people in St Austell went into mourning when the old boiler chimney began to be dismantled, brick by brick, in November 1980. It

was a thing of beauty - tall, elegant, tapering to slenderness, a typical Victorian decorative brick stack which had graced the skyline for nearly 90 years - but it had fallen from favour with local people since it started depositing clouds of sooty smuts onto their cars, houses, children, dogs and clean washing. Unable to cure the problem, the Brewery had to replace it with a 100ft steel stack in a different position, bypassing the underground flues. It works - it is efficient, clean, economical, sensible - but no one could ever accuse it of being beautiful. In 2001, with the advent of more fuel-efficient technology, it is being replaced by a 35ft stack and a single boiler system.

Slightly more nostalgia accompanied the passing of the Brewery steam hooter in 2000. No longer needed in an age when the constraints of old working practices have loosened, it was nonetheless a familiar and dependable feature of local life from Polgooth to Charlestown to Tregrehan (depending on the wind direction); a part of the aural landscape. It wasn't just the Brewery staff who stopped for crib when the 10 o'clock hooter went. Who knows how many lives revolved unconsciously around its regular wheezy blasts, and how many internal clocks were disorientated when it finally fell silent? *'We have relied on this wonderful sound so much'*, wrote a St Austell resident to the *Western Morning News*, *'especially the 7am hoot, but without the lunchtime and 4pm friendly sounds we feel quite lost.'*

As the new millennium approached, and more and more independent breweries ceased brewing in the face of competition from national and international brands, the Brewery had to reassess where it was and how it fitted in to the modern industry. Gone for ever was the era of thousands of small breweries scattered across the country, each with their own estate of pubs and a dependable local beer market. Enormous volumes were brewed back then because beer was practically a staple diet and the customer was not exactly faced with a vast array of alternatives when he walked into his local: you were either a mild man or a bitter man and that's the way you stayed. Today St Austell is one of around 35 independent regional family breweries still brewing, and in addition it faces a particular challenge common to all Cornish businesses reliant on wild fluctuations in seasonal demand. Yet to brew or not to brew was never really the question, for it has always been understood by everyone - the Board, the staff, the shareholders - that brewing is the very heart and soul of this company. Instead, the Brewery has recommitted itself to the art of brewing premium ales, with the focus on quality right the way through from raw materials to output and service.

In 1999 a new Head Brewer, Roger Ryman, was appointed by James Staughton and he brought with him a belief in the inherent strengths of regional breweries and a confidence in the power and value of a good product. *'Making beer is like making anything else. Take a steak for instance: if you've got a good piece of*

[continued on page 60]

The Brewing Process

Sometimes referred to as the world's second oldest profession, brewing in one form or other has long been an everyday part of life in the British Isles. The Roman writer Pliny wrote of the fondness of western Europeans for a drink made from corn and water: *'So exquisite is the cunning of mankind in gratifying their vicious appetites that they have thus invented a method to make water itself intoxicating.'* Another Roman wrote that Celts in Britain steeped and germinated grain, by which its spirits were excited and set free; it was then dried, ground, and infused in water when, after fermentation, it produced a pleasant, warming, strengthening and intoxicating liquor. Until the emergence of purpose-built brewhouses in the eighteenth century, brewing was largely a domestic activity carried out in farm and cottage kitchens, in monasteries, great houses, colleges and,

later, taverns. Beer was the everyday drink for all ages. Brewing was as normal an activity as baking bread and, like bread-making, the fundamental process remains much the same as it ever was even if the tools of the trade have changed with the times.

The traditional tower system of brewing, still in use at St Austell, starts with the initial ingredients being pumped or hoisted to the highest point of the brewery, and from here progress from one stage to the next is governed by the force of gravity.

MILLING: In the 1890 mill at the top of the tower, malted barley is ground to break down the outer walls of the grains to produce 'grist': a coarse flour.

ABOVE: *The mill.* RIGHT: *Mashing.* CENTRE RIGHT TOP: *Adding hops to the copper.*
CENTRE RIGHT BOTTOM: *Checking specific gravity during fermentation.*
FAR RIGHT: *Kegging.*

MASHING: In the mash tuns on the floor below the mill, the grist is mixed with 'liquor', as water is called throughout the brewing process, which has been heated to 74°C. The grist and liquor enter the mash tuns together at a temperature of around 65°C, heaving and plopping occasionally like porridge on a stove and smelling of hot sweet biscuits. The 'goods', as the grist and liquor mixture is known, now stand in the tuns for an hour, during which time a fermentable malty sugary solution is extracted from the grains.

SPARGING: After the stand, the goods are 'sparged' (sprayed with hot liquor which permeates down through the goods and extracts the malty sugars from them). The solution produced by sparging is known as 'sweet wort'; it is the colour of honey and tastes like malt syrup. Sparging continues until the required amount of wort has been drawn off from the bottom of the tuns, through brass taps, into the 'underback', from where it is pumped to the 'copper'. The spent grist is sold as cattle feed.

BOILING: The copper, a massive steam-heated cauldron, is where the hops are added to the wort and boiled for 1½ hours to extract bitterness from the hops, to sterilise the wort, and to remove any unwanted proteins. A portion of the hops is kept back and added at the end of the boil, to enhance the hoppy aroma of the beers. From the copper the 'hopped wort' passes through a 'hop back' where, after resting for ½ hour whilst the hops settle to the bottom, the wort then filters down through this bed of hops and is pumped to a 'wort receiver' before moving on to the cooling process. The spent hops are sold as fertiliser.

COOLING: This is a critical part of the process as the temperature of the wort needs to be driven down from around 90°C to 18°C before the yeast can be added. Once cooled, the wort is pumped to the fermenting vessels.

FERMENTING: Yeast is the magic ingredient of beer. This mysterious living fungus transforms the wort in spectacular fashion, the foaming head of the yeast on top of the wort being a striking indication of the frantic activity taking place beneath. The yeast's main job is to convert the sugar in the wort into alcohol and carbon dioxide. By tradition, the beer stays in the fermenting vessels for a week because *'any beer that has not been blessed by the Sabbath is deemed ungodly'*.

THE FINISHED PRODUCTS:
Traditional cask-conditioned beers - HSD, Tinners, Tribute, IPA, Dartmoor Best and XXXX Mild, plus the seasonal beers - are simply 'racked' (put into cask) from the fermenting vessels. They have 'finings' (made from the

swim bladder of the sturgeon) added to help the yeast to settle and produce a clear pint. IPA also has a small quantity of aromatic hops added to give a special dry hop flavour.

Keg beers - Duchy, Cornish Cream and Celtic Smooth - are put into a tank at cellar temperature after leaving the fermenting vessels, and left for a week to ten days. This enables the remaining yeast to ferment any residual sugars, thus creating natural condition. The beer is then passed through a chiller into a cold tank and held at -1°C for 48 hours, prior to filtering. The filter removes any suspended solids, and at this stage any adjustment needed to the carbon dioxide content is made. The beer is now pasteurised (sterilised) prior to kegging.

Bottled beers - Clouded Yellow and HSD - are sent by road tanker to a contract bottler, where the beer undergoes a similar process to kegging.

meat you can easily ruin it, but you'll never get a great steak out of a bad piece of meat. You have to start off with the best possible materials for brewing.' The key materials to get right, along with water and yeast, are malt and hops. The Brewery uses premium quality Maris Otter malt, some of which still comes from Tuckers Maltings in Newton Abbot (see pictures on pages 6/7) in keeping with company policy to use local suppliers where possible. Tuckers is a small business that celebrated its centenary in 2000; of all its original brewery customers back in 1900, St Austell Brewery is the only one which still exists. It is also vitally important to use the finest hops, and different varieties are used to impart different flavours to the beers. For HSD and Tinners, Fuggles and Goldings are used - traditional, old-fashioned English hops grown in Herefordshire - but with some of the newer beers Roger is experimenting with varieties from overseas, including New Zealand and America. *'For Tribute and IPA we use hops from Washington and Oregon - they have a very citrusy, tangy flavour which comes across in those beers, whereas English hops tend to be drier.'*

What is the popular image of a traditional Head Brewer? Someone in his fifties maybe, portly and grey-haired in a tweed jacket, a blunt no-nonsense character who likes a few drinks, a bit domineering in the brewhouse perhaps, someone to be feared as well as respected. In the realm of mash tuns and fermenting vessels, he is king. There is an ancient mystique surrounding the brewing of beer; it even has its own language peppered with Anglo-Saxon words - wort, grist, liquor, the goods, finings, racking, sparging - which is impenetrable to outsiders. Roger Ryman does not exactly fit the picture of the typical Head Brewer of the past, and as for his profession's tendency to shroud itself in mystery, he says that *'brewers are second only to car mechanics for making something simple seem complicated'.*

FAR RIGHT: *Mash tun.*

Tribute

Tribute started life as Daylight Robbery, a short-term seasonal beer brewed to celebrate the total eclipse of the sun in August 1999. Its phenomenal success came as something of a surprise, not least to Roger Ryman: *'It was the first new beer I'd brewed at St Austell. I was used to producing new beers every two months at Maclays [the Scottish brewery where Roger had been Assistant Head Brewer]; they were made, they sold and we moved on. With Daylight I just thought that's a nice pint, that's good, and then it just went ballistic. It had a great name and the timing was good, but a month after its launch it was the Brewery's best selling beer and sales carried on like that for the rest of the summer and into autumn.'* Daylight had made itself indispensable; by virtue of its success and popularity it promoted itself from the ephemeral to the permanent and in 2001 it was relaunched as one of the Brewery's core brands under its new name: Tribute.

Clouded Yellow

Like Daylight Robbery, the success of Clouded Yellow took everyone by surprise; indeed you could almost say it caught them on the hop. This distinctive beer, in the style of a German wheat beer, was one of several experimental one-off brews created by Roger for the first Celtic Beer Festival in 1999. Just two barrels were made and it went down well at the festival under the unofficial name of Hagar the Horrible. *'Then the Tesco Beer Challenge came up'*, as Roger recalled, *'and they were looking for new innovative beers so I bunged some in a bottle and sent it off just for fun.'* It was with a mixture of alarm and delight that he discovered it had won first prize and the Brewery had just five weeks to develop it commercially and get it ready for Tesco to distribute nationwide through its supermarkets. Moreover, no-one else in the Brewery management knew he had entered it in the competition, and it didn't even have a name. Eventually they picked Clouded Yellow from a book of British butterflies because it suited the look and style of the beer and they wanted a bright, summery image on the label. In addition, they liked the apt description of the butterfly as *'a migrant: it is most common in the South but reaches all parts of the British Isles'.* As St Austell's first nationally-distributed beer it has gone down very well; it has won many plaudits including coming top in a *Which?* magazine tasting of bottle-fermented beers (*'a golden, refreshing beer, our panellists praised it for its typical wheat beer flavours such as spice, apples and particularly bananas'*).

The unforgettable smell of a brewery at work

Lynn Pearson identified in *British Breweries: an Architectural History* what she calls *'the emotional impact of that distinctive hoppy aroma'* and no-one describes this better than Dr A.L. Rowse who attended St Austell Grammar School in the early 1900s:

'...And then there was that more exotic scent from the Brewery next door, of malt or hops or of I do not know what aromatic spices they used in brewing, which the west wind blew across our playing fields, enveloping the school in its warm, soft, sweet, drowsy, liquorous smell, that insinuated itself into the passages and corridors and classrooms, came in puffs at the windows, lurked heavily about the lower quarters of the school - and, in short, so wound itself into my mind that often when I think of those school days the memory of that nostalgic smell is entwined with them.' (From *A Cornish Childhood*).

Yet there is no escaping the feeling, when you catch that sweet and heady smell on the wind on brewing days, that something magical like alchemy must be going on inside those brewhouse walls. Part of this mystique comes from the fact that brewing is both an art and a science. As Roger says, it is *'a life science. All the basic processes of life are there in brewing. A lot of early research by Louis Pasteur and others, breaking down the actual biochemistry of life, was done in breweries. But it is also an art in that there's always a place for flair, and the good thing about working in a brewery like St Austell is that you've got the scope to use it.'*

Since Roger's arrival the Brewery has made a long-term commitment to its four core draught ales - HSD, Tinners, Tribute and IPA - opening up the future possibility of featuring on the national stage in what is a growing market for premium guest beers from high-quality reputable regional brewers. It also now has a seasonal beer programme based on six new short-term brews a year which are particularly popular with the free trade. In addition the Brewery still produces XXXX Mild which won a CAMRA Best Beer award in 1990 and is one of the few remaining draught milds still being brewed in the country. In keg, Duchy is still going strong, alongside the popular newcomers Cornish Cream and Celtic Smooth. Two bottled beers are also produced, with the bottling taking place at Brakspear's and Redruth since the closure of the bottling line in 1995: HSD and the award-winning Clouded Yellow.

In December 1999 the Brewery hosted its first Celtic Beer Festival, featuring draught ales and lagers from Cornwall, Scotland, Ireland, Wales, the Isle of Man and Brittany, and music from Cornish bands and choirs. Held in the atmospheric surroundings of the Brewery cellars and the old bonded warehouse, linked together by the tunnel, the festival was a hugely successful celebration of Celtic pride and excellent brewing. It has since become an annual event.

In April 2000 James Staughton became Managing Director of the Brewery on Piers Thompson's retirement. Piers in turn succeeded James's father, David Staughton, as Chairman. As Walter Hicks's great-great grandson, James is the fifth generation of the Hicks family to be actively involved in running St Austell Brewery, along with his cousin Piers Thompson junior who joined in 1993. Another cousin, William Michelmore, was appointed to the Board in 1996 as a non-executive director. This is a remarkable dynastic achievement for any business, and it is at the heart of the Brewery's success as one of the great Cornish

The HSD story

Probably St Austell Brewery's most famous brand, and certainly its most infamous, Hicks Special Draught started life in 1975. The possibility of producing a *'good strength and comparatively expensive Draught Bitter from the Wood'* was first discussed by George Luck, Piers Thompson and the Head Brewer Alan Izat two years earlier. In the summer of '75 the Board agreed that Alan's *'experimental brews of a high-quality naturally conditioned draught beer at 1050° should be tried out in 20-30 tied houses on a pilot basis. It would be called "Hicks's Special Draught" and it was envisaged that it would sell at 26p a pint'.* Despite its subsequent success, which today sometimes sees it outstripping Tinners as the Brewery's best seller, HSD was a tricky brew at first and had rather a rocky start. Adam Luck, who had just started at the Brewery, remembers it vividly: *'it was troublesome, problematical, difficult for landlords to handle...so we withdrew it to get it right and then relaunched it the following year and it's been a huge success ever since. It's now considered to be our key brand because it is so unusual - it is markedly different to other beers.'* Hicks Special Draught was produced in half-pint bottles as Jubilee Ale in 1977, to celebrate the Queen's Silver Jubilee, and today is contract bottled for the Brewery as HSD.

HSD's distinctive taste and *'a certain reputation as one that's going to knock you over'*, as Roger Ryman puts it, have given it something of a cult following over the years and spawned a number of nicknames including Hicks's Sudden Death and High Speed Diesel. The Cornish love it, but is the rest of the country ready for HSD?

The dying art of the brewery cooper: Bill Hockin (right c.1935), father of Company Secretary Clifford Hockin, was Head Cooper at the Brewery from the early years of the twentieth century; Llew Jones (below) ran the cooper's shop from 1977 until his retirement in 2001. Interviewed by the Western Morning News *in 1995 to celebrate his 40 years in the coopering trade, Llew explained how it took him about a day to make a nine gallon firkin:* 'We mainly use old hogshead rum barrels from Guyana which we cut up to make smaller casks. That way we don't waste good wood, and the steaming and hot fires – which are part of the making process – help to disperse the rum flavouring of the wood. The skills of the cooper still lie in the use of some 22 tools. All the work is done by eye, I don't measure anything.'

companies. Its essential stability comes from this continuity not just of family ownership but of family management. As well as having a more remote relationship as shareholders, Walter's descendents have always worked in the Brewery and for the Brewery, and therein lies the strength. Like those Victorian gardeners who planted trees for another generation to enjoy, the Managing Director sees himself as a custodian; rather than sweating whatever he can out of the company for short-term gain, he takes the long view, with a perspective shaped by both the past and the future.

The Brewery Visitor Centre, opened in 1992. The centre includes a video presentation area, an off-licence, souvenir and gift shop and a sample bar. Guided tours of the Brewery are available - please telephone to book. The Visitor Centre may also be hired for meetings, conferences, parties etc.

Messages of congratulation

To me the story of St Austell Brewery embodies the spirit of Cornwall. Like Cornwall, the Brewery is a close-knit community with family origins. It has resisted being subsumed by larger concerns, and established its good name by trading on quality and distinctiveness.

Now, as Cornwall begins to re-invent itself using a vigorous Objective One programme and world-class features like Eden, Gaia, Falmouth Maritime and the Tate St Ives, we need more than ever to salute our successful businesses.

Companies which have prospered in Cornwall need to be highlighted as examples of what can be achieved. St Austell Brewery has not only gained a well-deserved reputation for fine products, but has also helped to 'brand' Cornwall using a strong corporate image on its 150 pubs and hotels, as well as diversifying into tourism attractions with its fascinating visitor centre.

I am thrilled to be able to 'raise a glass' to your success, and to say a hearty 'well done' to all the staff via the pages of this 150th Anniversary book.

Pippa Englefield, Leader of the Council,
Cornwall County Council.

I would like to offer my congratulations to St Austell Brewery on its 150th anniversary. It brings great credit to Cornwall as one of the few independent breweries left in the country and it is good to have a family business continuing which gives employment to so many Cornish people.

I hope that in 150 years time it will still be flourishing as a large Cornish employer. We all look forward to many more years of being able to visit a truly Cornish pub!

With many congratulations to all the staff and tenants of such a successful Cornish business.

Lady Mary Holborow, Lord Lieutenant of Cornwall.

When the Campaign for Real Ale was formed back in 1973, it was in response to an accelerating decline in the availability and quality of real ale around the country. Breweries were being taken over and closed down at an alarming rate, and the industry was becoming more and more dominated by the 'big six' national brewers who seemed to lose interest in cask conditioned beers, preferring to turn out large quantities of pressurised keg beers which were beginning to threaten real ale with near-extinction in many areas of the country.

Cornwall was at that time considered to be relatively fortunate in this respect, having two regional-sized family owned brewers who at least had some commitment to real ale, but as the history of Devenish shows, even they were not ultimately safe from the take-over and asset-stripping exercise that was rampant in the industry in those days. Fortunately, St Austell Brewery survived, and eventually thrived, and as far as CAMRA is concerned, are to be congratulated on a self-evident commitment to an interesting range of decent, tasty ales, and to ensuring that they reach the customer in prime condition.

The Cornwall branch of CAMRA has always been concerned that St Austell, with nearly a quarter of the county's pubs, should remain as an independent bulwark against take-over by a large predatory brewer, and we offer our heartiest congratulations to the brewery for arriving at the first 150 year milestone in good shape and with an excellent range of ales, and good pubs in which to drink them.

Cheers!

Rod Davis, Chairman, Cornwall Branch of CAMRA.

I remember St Austell Brewery. It was right next door to the then Grammar School and the smell I can still remember was distinctive and overpowering. It was also a place into which a couple of entrepreneurial school-friends of mine would sneak of a morning to pick up dog-ends dropped by the employees. The tobacco from these was then rolled up into 'new' cigarettes and passed around behind the bike shed. They tasted, as you would expect, awful – quite different from the taste, the glorious taste, of the pints and pints of St Austell Extra I consumed during those happy days in Cornwall.

John Nettles, actor (past pupil of St Austell Grammar School).

Cornwall boasts many great success stories – but few can be so emphatic and inspiring as that of St Austell Brewery. Its growth into one of the county's leading employers, and its survival as an independent regional brewer during years of takeover and amalgamation add up to a truly inspiring tale.

The fact that it is a traditional family business, built on distinctiveness and local employment and sourcing, makes this milestone achievement all the more impressive. Even in this day and age, when it seems boundaries are forever being pushed back and everything is changing at lightning speed, St Austell Brewery's continuing strength emphasises the enduring values of tradition, high standards and local involvement.

Indeed, we could all learn so much from this success story. If there's one thing I have learnt from some 20 years at the sharp end of South West business, it is that many of the solutions to our greatest problems – our greatest challenges – can be overcome right here on our own doorstep. We can spend too much time looking too far afield for answers, when so many of the skills and characteristics we need are to be found here among our own people.

Certainly, St Austell Brewery epitomises this spirit and all that is good about Cornwall and its heritage. I say 'cheers' to all those who made, and continue to make, such an outstanding feat possible. May they prosper for another 150 years!

Cairns Boston, Chairman, South West Tourism and Cornwall College.

It used to be said that families went from clogs to riches and back to clogs again in three generations. Nowadays the average lifespan of a public company is about one generation, before it fails or is taken over. So it is really remarkable that St Austell Brewery has not only survived 150 years, but has prospered too. The reason is not hard to see: successive owners have invested in the local community, directly and in many unsung indirect ways as well. This has paid off in terms of the loyalty of thousands of 'regulars' in pubs across the county of Cornwall.

Here's to the next 150 years.

Lady Banham, High Sheriff of Cornwall 2000-2001.

Wherever you are in Cornwall you are never far from a St Austell House. There's something deeply comforting about the name, as if it stood for virtues as deeply rooted in Cornwall as the granite from which most of the ale houses were built. It's not fussy, or trendy, in fact it is reassuringly old-fashioned. This is staff of life stuff, not designer froth.

The HQ in St Austell is austere and unforgiving with no concession to frills, its prison-like quality appropriate to the names of its famous brews: Tinners, Wreckers, Daylight etc. Most importantly, it sits on the bluff above the once quaint market and mining town that gave it its name. The brewery gives the place a character and connection with the past that compensates, in some small part, for the ache of bereavement through the last fifty years as first tin and then clay began their contraction.

That was many pints ago; now we have a bright future to look forward to and I would like to wish all at St Austell Brewery well as they seek to uphold a name of which they can be justly proud.

Tim Smit, Chief Executive, Eden Project.

In the years we have been associated with St Austell Brewery we have always found them to be such nice people to deal with, from the directors, brewery staff and draymen. we regard them as friends who are on your side, to make the tenant/brewery partnership work and to benefit both sides. Congratulations to St Austell Brewery on the last 150 years and let us all work towards the 200. Keep it in the family, well done.

Rosie and Peter Angwin, tenants of the Star Inn, St Just since 1984.

My first taste of St Austell beer was 35 years ago in the charming Plume of Feathers at Portscatho. A Pint of Boys soon became a way of life, and there were many charming hostelries of St Austell Brewery to seek out. On joining CAMRA as one of the early Cornish branch members I soon became familiar with the Brewery, and it remains one of the few genuine regional brewers who rely on tradition without losing sight of the changing demands of the consumer. I wish you all well in the future as you enter your third century of trading.

Ivor Bowditch, Community and Public Relations Manager, Imerys.

I have fond memories of St Austell Brewery and its association in particular with East Cornwall, especially with my home village of Pelynt, the home of the Trelawny family. When the promotion of Trelawny's Ale was inaugurated, the Bishop of Truro came to the church, blessed the cask, and of course there was a splendid rendition of 'Trelawny'.

The brewery has been extremely supportive of our County Rugby team, and we gratefully acknowledge their generosity in donating casks of beer when the County Council hosts the victorious County Champions in successful seasons. This, served with a proper pasty from the Lizard, makes it truly a time of Cornish celebration. We are looking forward to the next such occasion!

Jim Philp, Chairman, Cornwall County Council.

May I congratulate St Austell Brewery on its 150th anniversary. On January 18th this year the Cornish Guardian celebrated its 100th anniversary so it is wonderful to have two such fine Cornish institutions reaching significant landmarks in 2001.

St Austell Brewery plays a leading role in the economy of Cornwall and a leading role in quenching the thirst of many of its inhabitants. The brewery is to be congratulated on maintaining its independent status in an industry that is dominated by huge multi-national companies.

Keep up the good work – and long may you brew!

Alan Cooper, Managing Editor, The Cornish Guardian.

What a great achievement. Congratulations to everyone at the Brewery and at all your 150 public houses and hotels. At a time when our economy is being assaulted by the massive corporate and international conglomerates, your accomplishment is all the greater, keeping skills, livelihood and employment in our rural and town communities. Even better, you have a brand that we are all proud of. The brewery has never lost its links with the local and with Cornwall. Long may your success last.

Oliver Baines, Director, Cornwall Rural Community Council.

The distinctiveness of Cornwall, and its way of life, is represented by many things, some of which combine to great effect.

The traditional black and gold signboards of St Austell Brewery's houses reassure the traveller throughout Cornwall, never more so than after a rejuvenating but thirsty coastal walk. More than 40% of Cornwall's incomparable coastline is now protected and opened up by the National Trust and its long-running Neptune Coastline Campaign. In 1966 the Brewery gave the infant Neptune a wonderful christening present by making possible the purchase of Gribbin Head on St Austell Bay, most appropriately as it is an eye-catching feature of the view from the company's boardroom window.

Long may these two Cornish 'institutions' prosper distinctively together.

Peter Mansfield, The National Trust's Director for Cornwall.

In a world which is growing smaller, and yet at the same time in which globalisation seems to take things over, what we are discovering is the importance of the local, and that word of course has a double meaning. The local can be the pub or it can be the area in which we live. I think one of the problems about modern living is that so many people are dislocated out of their place and to have a family business like the St Austell Brewery there in the middle of Cornwall is a reminder to all of us how important a local business like a brewery is, not just because it provides beer, etc, but because it is a symbol of the local, of that which is near at hand, and which people can recognise and feel they have an investment in. It contributes a great deal to Cornish life in various ways and I myself always enjoy tasting its products!

Bill Ind, The Bishop of Truro.

St Austell Brewery is one of the things that makes life in Cornwall such fun. From the cliff tops at Treen to the coastal inlet at Restronguet, it's always enjoyable to introduce visitors to the lovely locations, interesting local flavour and genuine Cornish hospitality of a St Austell pub. St Austell Brewery is an impressive example of a local specialist surviving and prospering in an increasingly faceless and corporate world.

Daphne Skinnard, BBC Radio Cornwall.

Working the Cornish farm on which I was born, one of the small things that has punctuated my life with a pleasing, touching sense of continuity has been the occasional discovery of a Walter Hicks bottle, thrown in the hedge after crib by men harvesting, ploughing and tilling the same field 100 years ago. Those thick, green, mud-encrusted bottles are a sign that St Austell Brewery has been rooted in the everyday life of Cornwall for a long time.

It still plays a proudly local and distinctive role. On behalf of Kneehigh, which has enjoyed the Brewery's support and sponsorship, I would like to salute another Cornish institution and raise a glass to St Austell Brewery's past and future.

Rose Barnecut, Chairman, Kneehigh Theatre Company.

A hundred and fifty years young – well done! It was in 1959 that I drank my first pint of St Austell Ale and I have enjoyed it regularly since then. Cornwall needs innovative, successful and quality businesses like yours and I wish everybody at St Austell Brewery all the very best for the next 150 years.

Cheers!

Peter Davies, Chief Executive, Cornwall County Council.

Cornwall is rightly proud of its identity, history and culture – and in any area there can be little more important than the local pint of real ale! Closed tin mines, farming in crisis, fishermen without fish – that is all part of modern Cornwall it seems; but the good news is there too, and whilst everybody will have a different view on their favourite pint, for me nothing beats a jug of Tinners! Not only that, but plenty of the St Austell Brewery pubs still retain not just the genuine feel of a traditional Cornish pub, but the genuine clientele too.

Sadly there are very few parts of the country now where the local beer is still brewed in the local brewery – but St Austell Brewery remains just that, and long may it thrive.

Matthew Taylor, MP for Truro and St Austell.

What comes to mind when you think of Cornwall? The glories of its natural environment, perhaps, the ancient history, exquisite church architecture or the many fine achievements of Cornish men and women through the ages. You might think of the rich diversity of local foods and recipes and the warm hospitality of its many historic pubs, or you may simply recognise the unique culture of Cornwall that helps to set this special part of Britain into a category of its own.

In short, the people of Cornwall have so much of which to be genuinely and truly proud and therefore now and again a moment or two of recognition and celebration is entirely appropriate! To my mind the St Austell Brewery Company falls admirably into this category, especially as this year marks the 150th anniversary of the founding of this prestigious local company – indeed one of Cornwall's oldest and most prestigious.

Today St Austell Brewery, with an annual turnover of some £50 million, employs more than 880 people and owns some 150 public houses and hotels in Cornwall and Devon. It is still very much a family concern and is justifiably proud to be one of the few remaining independent regional breweries in the country. The Brewery is widely recognised for the quality of its beers and for its commitment to highest all round standards, both for product and customer care. As such it is a big player in our all-important tourist industry and beyond any shadow of a doubt adds immeasurably to the distinctiveness that is Cornwall.

If ever an organisation in Cornwall has pursued a philosophy of excellence it is St Austell Brewery and I wish it all possible and continued success.

Michael Galsworthy, Chairman, In Pursuit of Excellence.

BREWERY STAFF 2000

I wish to thank Liz Luck and Laurence Sutherland for writing and designing this wonderful book. When I see our history in print it brings home to me how similar my grandfather's philosophy to life and his business work ethic are to mine. It is fitting that his close partner should have been George Luck whose son Adam is my colleague and co-Board Director today.

On looking at our past we recognise we have much to be proud of and grateful for. Certainly our predecessors have much to teach us. We aim to build on the strong management and business acumen of Piers Thompson and Peter Voelcker. Their skills helped bring us such success over the last two decades and as we celebrate our 150th year we look back on the values of Walter, Hester but particularly my grandfather Egbert Barnes. Once more we commit openly to values so similar to those they embraced.

James Staughton, left, with Adam Luck.

As Managing Director my vision for St Austell Brewery is to achieve the ultimate in business success - a happy and fulfilled team working together for the good of the Company, our customers and the community. In line with this vision, I am proud to be able to announce that in our 150th year the Company has earned the prestigious 'Investors in People' award.

As a family of shareholders we are committed in our loyalty and devotion to St Austell Brewery and its prosperity, to the development of the workforce and to the satisfaction of its customers. A very big thank you to everyone associated with the Brewery over the last 150 years and may we all continue to prosper throughout the 21st century and beyond by continuing to invest in our people, our products and our licensed houses.

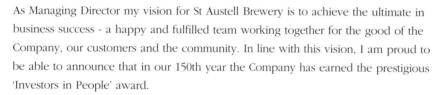

James Staughton
MANAGING DIRECTOR

APPENDIX I - **Directors of the Company**

Walter Hicks	1910/16	Chairman	
Walter Hicks junior	1910/11		
Hester Parnall	1911/39	Chairman 1916/39	
Reginald Barnes	1916/35		
Christopher Ellis	1934/50		
Egbert Barnes	1935/79	Chairman 1939/79	President 1979/87
Kenneth Moore	1939/76		
Arthur Payne	1939/42	Managing	
Claude Aylwin	1942/47	Managing	
Scott Seaward	1944/60		
George Luck	1948/79	Managing	
Leonard Minchin	1952/57		
David Payne	1959/63		
Ian Turnbull	1961/63		
David Staughton	1963/2000	Chairman 1979/2000	
Piers Thompson	1967/	Managing 1979/2000	Chairman 2000/
Peter Voelcker	1967/		
Michael Ruthven	1987/2000		
Adam Luck	1988/		
James Staughton	1988/	Managing 2000/	
William Michelmore	1996/		

Bold type: members of the Hicks family.

APPENDIX II - **Hicks family tree**

WALTER HICKS 1829/1916

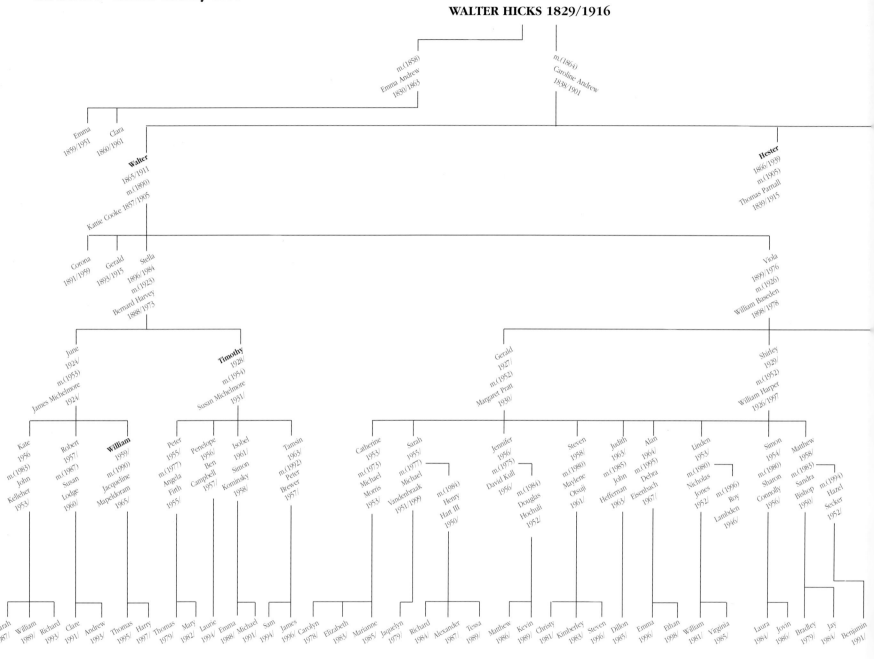

m.(1858)
Emma Andrew
1830/1863

m.(1864)
Caroline Andrew
1838/1901

Emma
1859/1951

Clara
1860/1961

Walter
1865/1911
m.(1890)
Kattie Cocke 1857/1905

Hester
1866/1939
m.(1905)
Thomas Parnall
1839/1915

Corona
1891/1959

Gerald
1893/1915

Stella
1896/1984
m.(1923)
Bernard Harvey
1888/1973

Viola
1899/1976
m.(1926)
William Baseden
1898/1978

June
1924/
m.(1953)
James Michelmore
1924/

Timothy
1928/
m.(1954)
Susan Michelmore
1931/

Gerald
1927/
m.(1952)
Margaret Pratt
1930/

Shirley
1929/
m.(1952)
William Harper
1926/1997

Kate
1956
m.(1983)
John
Kelleher
1953/

Robert
1957/
m.(1987)
Susan
Lodge
1960/

William
1959/
m.(1990)
Jacqueline
Mapeldoram
1965/

Peter
1955/
m.(1977)
Angela
Firth
1955/

Penelope
1956/
Ben
Campbell
1957/

Isobel
1961/
Simon
Kominsky
1958/

Tamsin
1963/
m.(1992)
Peter
Brewer
1957/

Catherine
1953/
m.(1973)
Michael
Morris
1953/

Sarah
1955/
m.(1977)
Michael
Vandenbraak
1951/1999

m.(1984)
Henry
Hart III
1950/

Jennifer
1956/
m.(1975)
David Kull
1956/

m.(1984)
Douglas
Hochuli
1952/

Steven
1958/
m.(1980)
Maylene
Otsuji
1961/

Judith
1963/
m.(1985)
John
Heffernan
1963/

Alan
1964/
m.(1995)
Debra
Eisenbach
1967/

Linden
1953/
m.(1980)
Nicholas
Jones
1952/

m.(1996)
Roy
Lambden
1946/

Simon
1954/
m.(1980)
Sharon
Connolly
1956/

Matthew
1958/
m.(1983)
Sandra
Bishop
1950/

m.(1994)
Hazel
Secker
1952/

Sarah
1987/

William
1989/

Richard
1993/

Clare
1991/

Andrew
1993/

Thomas
1995/

Harry
1997/

Thomas
1979/

Mary
1982/

Laurie
1994/

Emma
1988/

Michael
1991/

Sam
1994/

James
1996/

Carolyn
1978/

Elizabeth
1983/

Marianne
1985/

Jacquelyn
1979/

Richard
1984/

Alexander
1987/

Tessa
1989/

Matthew
1986/

Kevin
1989/

Christy
1981/

Kimberley
1983/

Steven
1996/

Dillon
1985/

Emma
1996/

Ethan
1998/

William
1981/

Virginia
1985/

Laura
1984/

Jovin
1986/

Bradley
1979/

Jay
1984/

Benjamin
1991/

Bold type: members of the Hicks family directly involved in the management of the Brewery.

Mary 1869/1954 m.(1896) **Reginald G Barnes** 1869/1935 Susan 1870/1945 Caroline 1872/1954 Margaret 1873/1957 Kate 1875/1955 m.(1907) Jack Hoyle 1882/1962 George 1880/1954 m.(1917) Nancy St-de-Croix 1877/1967

Egbert 1898/1987 m.(1934) Ruth Blezard 1901/1981 Hester 1900/1988 m.(1931) Piers Thompson 1893/1969 Elizabeth 1904/1990 m.(1934) George Fraser 1887/1970 Ruth 1910/1987 m.(1935) Paul Voelcker 1901/1959

Gillian 1930 m.(1955) Rodney Curry 1928/ Richard 1932/1993 m.(1958) Jacqueline Luke 1938/ Olivia 1936/ m.(1957) **David Staughton** 1931/ David 1940/ m.(1965) Ursula Pitman 1944/ Roger 1933/ m.(1959) Suzanne Holmes 1934/ m.(1986) Margaret Wood 1948/ Deborah 1936/ m.(1966) David Varden 1927/ **Piers** 1937/ m.(1966) Victoria Thwaites 1944/ Robert 1935/ m.(1964) Sarah Peck 1941/ Patrick 1938/ m.(1975) Patricia Frost 1948/ **Peter** 1938/ m.(1978) Alison Edwards 1948/ Celia 1943/ m.(1982) James Milnes Gaskell 1937/ Rosemary 1947/

...ick 1960 ...(1979) ...nda Scott Alexandra 1960/ Tessa 1961 m.(1986) Peter Stock 1959/ Ben 1964 m.(1990) Tracy Bayliss 1962/ Virginia 1969/ Julia 1962 m.(1991) Michael Clancy 1962/ Alexander 1966/ Thomas 1969/ **James** 1959 m.(1995) Rebecca Trafford 1963/ m.(2000) Emma Minter-Kemp 1960/ Julia 1960/ Fiona 1963 m.(1991) Clive Roberts 1958/ Gerard 1968 m.(1996) Jane Larroucau 1968/ Robert 1969/ Adam 1950 Jessica Datta 1952/ Lucy 1962/ Hugo 1966 Sophie Friend 1963/ Clara 1988/ Richard 1967 m.(1998) Ashley Cameron 1972/ James 1969 m.(1998) Janine Anketell 1967/ Annabel 1968 m.(1998) Jonty White 1965/ **Piers** 1971/ Emily 1983/ Fiona 1965/ David 1966/ Alexandra 1979/ Camilla 1981/ Sophie 1981/ Humphrey 1980/ Arthur 1988/ Charles 1983/ Anna 1985/

...es ...1 Charlotte 1983/ Felix 1987/ India 1994/ Milo 1999/ Torran 2000/ Jack 1991/ Finn 1997/ Oscar 1999/ Sabine 1998/ Emma 2000/ Olivia 1993/ Katrina 1996/ Christian 1998/ Benedict 2000/ Celeste 1988/ Coralie 1991/ Alexander 2000/ Archie 1999/ Matilda 2001/

APPENDIX III - **Pubs and hotels owned by the Brewery in 2001**

Name	Date acquired	Name	Date acquired
Abbey Inn, Buckfast	1996	Crown Inn, Goldsithney	1911
Angarrack Inn, Angarrack	1935	Crown Inn, St Ewe	1917
Atlantic Inn, St Mary's	1988	Crows Nest, Darite	
Badger Inn, Lelant		(formerly The Sun Inn)	1905
(formerly Lelant Hotel)	1935	Darlington Inn, Camelford	1923
Barley Sheaf, Bodmin	1898	Dolphin Inn, Grampound	1916
Barley Sheaf, Liskeard	1910	Dolphin Inn, Penzance	1935
Barley Sheaf, St Columb	1889	Double Decker Bars, Looe	1962
Bettle and Chisel, Delabole		Duke of Cornwall, Mount Charles,	
(formerly Delabole Inn)	1925	St Austell	1889
Bishop and Wolf Inn, St Mary's	1958	Earl of Chatham, Lostwithiel	1926
Brass Monkey, Teignmouth	1996	Earl of St Vincent, Egloshayle	1922
Blue Anchor, Fraddon	1939	Edgcumbe Arms, Cremyll	1994 (leasehold)
Buccaneer Inn, Torquay	1996	Falcon Inn, St Mawgan	1988 (leasehold)
Bucket of Blood, Phillack		Falmouth Arms, Ladock	1893
(formerly New Inn)	1935	Falmouth Packet, Rosudgeon	1935
Bugle Inn, Bugle	1920 (freehold 1971)	Farmers Arms, St Merryn	1951
Carbeile Inn, Torpoint	1984	Ferryboat Inn, Helford Passage	1987 (leasehold)
Carlyon Arms, St Austell	1929	Fire Engine Inn, Marazion	1935
Cellars Bar, Teignmouth	1996	Fishermans Arms, Newlyn	1935
Central Inn, Newquay	1902	Fishermans Arms, Plymouth	1991
Commercial Inn, St Dennis	1897	The Fort, Newquay	1997
Copley Arms, Hessenford	1959	Fountain Inn, Mevagissey	1883
Cornish Arms, Bodmin	1919	Fountain Inn, Newbridge	1935
Cornish Arms, Hayle	1935	Fountain Tavern, Penzance	1935
Cornish Arms, St Blazey	1891	Fox and Hounds, Comford	1949
Cornish Arms, St Merryn	1926 (freehold 1982)	Four Lords, St Blazey	1904
Cornubia Hotel, Hayle	1935	Four Winds, Falmouth	1954
		George and Dragon, Bodmin	1922

Name	Date acquired	Name	Date acquired
Globe Hotel, Bude	1905 (leasehold)	Lugger Inn, Polruan	1938
Golden Lion, Menherion	1923	Masons Arms, Camelford	1923
Golden Lion, Port Isaac	1922	Masons Arms, Falmouth	1918
Great Western Hotel, Newquay	1985	Mechanics Arms, Plymouth	1991
Grenville Arms, Nanpean	1911 (freehold 1984)	Mill on the Exe, Exeter	1994
Harbour Inn, Padstow (formerly Commercial Hotel)	1922	Mount Ambrose Inn, Mount Ambrose	1935
		Napoleon Inn, Boscastle	1993
Harbour Inn, Porthleven	1985	New Inn, Park Bottom	1935
Hawkins Arms, Probus	1919	New Inn, Tywardreath	1932
Heron Inn, Malpas (formerly Park Hotel)	1930	New Inn, Veryan	1943
		North Inn, Pendeen	1935
Hewas Inn, Sticker	1927	O'Callaghan's, St Austell (formerly Sun Inn)	1909
Holmbush Inn, St Austell	1929		
King of Prussia, Fowey	1895 (freehold 1989)	Old Custom House, Padstow	1989
Kings Arms, Bridges, Luxulyan	1909	Old Inn, Ludgvan	1935
Kings Arms, Lostwithiel	1922	Old Smithy, Ivybridge	1996
Kings Arms, Marazion	1935	Oystercatcher, Polzeath (formerly Polzeath Hotel)	1963
Kings Arms, Paul	1935		
Kings Arms, St Just	1935	Pandora Inn, Restronguet	1982
Kings Arms, St Stephen	1915 (freehold 1927)	Par Inn, Par	1926
Kings Head, Lane	2000	Pedn-Olva Hotel, St Ives	1999
Lanivet Inn, Lanivet	1893	Pirate Inn, Falmouth	1988 (leasehold)
Lemon Arms, Mylor	1920	Pityme Inn, Pityme	1998
Lifeboat Inn, St Ives	1964 (freehold 1997)	Plume of Feathers, Portscatho	1921
Logan Rock, Treen	1958 (freehold 1991)	Poachers, Roche (formerly the Commercial Inn]	1914 (leasehold)
London Inn, Padstow	1907		
London Inn, Summercourt	1944	Polgooth Inn, Polgooth	1916
Lugger Inn, Fowey	1930 (freehold 1989)	Queens Head, St Stephen	1919

Name	Date acquired	Name	Date acquired
Queens Hotel, St Ives	1967	St Kew Inn, St Kew	1922
Radjel Inn, Pendeen (formerly Boscaswell Inn)	1935	Swan Hotel, Wadebridge (formerly Commercial Hotel)	1922
Railway Inn, Illogan	1935	Tap and Barrel, Exeter	1994
Revenue Inn, Plymouth	1991	Three Tuns, Penryn	1943
Ring of Bells, Bishopsteignton	1996	Travellers Rest, Trevarrian	1935
Rising Sun, St Mawes	1930	Turnpike Inn, Connor Downs	1935
Rodney Inn, Helston	1935	Tyacks Hotel, Camborne	1917
Rolle Quay Inn, Barnstaple	2000	Victoria Bars, Newquay	1917
Royal Standard, Hayle	1935	Victoria Inn, Roche	1943
Russell Inn, Polruan	1925	Victoria Inn, Salcombe	2001
Safe Harbour Hotel, Fowey (formerly Commercial Hotel)	1903 (freehold 1982)	Victoria Inn, Threemilestone	1944
Sawles Arms, Carthew	1919	Waterfront, Plymouth	1998 (leasehold)
Seven Stars, St Austell	1863 (freehold 1925)	Weavers, Bodmin	1983
Sheaf of Wheat, St Ives	1904	Welcome Home Inn, Par	1913
Ship Hotel, Looe	1960	Wellington Hotel, St Just	1935
Ship Inn, Fowey	1891 (freehold 1989)	Western Inn, St Austell	1943 (freehold 1962)
Ship Inn, Mevagissey	1896	Western Hotel, Plymouth	1991
Ship Inn, Mousehole	1901	Western Hotel, St Ives	1948
Ship Inn, Pentewan	1943	Westward Inn, Ivybridge	1996
Ship Inn, Portloe	1909 (freehold 1947)	White Hart Hotel, St Austell	1911
Shipwrights Inn, Padstow	1965	Wig and Pen, Truro (formerly Star Inn)	1926
Sir Humphry Davy, Penzance (formerly St Johns House)	1910 (freehold 1926)	William Cookworthy, St Austell	1969
Star Inn, St Just	1935 (freehold 1979)	William IVth, Truro	1898
St Agnes Hotel, St Agnes (formerly Paull's Hotel)	1923	Wodehouse Arms, Falmouth	1913
		Yacht Inn, Penzance	1935